I AM A CAMERA

BY JOHN VAN DRUTEN

ADAPTED FROM "THE BERLIN STORIES"
OF CHRISTOPHER ISHERWOOD

WITH PREFACE BY THE AUTHOR

A PLAY IN THREE ACTS

DRAMATISTS
PLAY SERVICE
INC.

SPECIAL NOTE

I Am a Camera was first presented by Gertrude Macy, in association with Walter Starcke, at the Empire Theatre, New York City, on November 28, 1951. It was staged by Mr. van Druten and the setting was by Boris Aronson. The cast was as follows:

CHRISTOPHER ISHERWOOD .... William Prince
FRAULEIN SCHNEIDER .... Olga Fabian
FRITZ WENDEL .... Martin Brooks
SALLY BOWLES .... Julie Harris
NATALIA LANDAUER .... Marian Winters
CLIVE MORTIMER .... Edward Andrews
MRS. WATSON-COURTNEIDGE .... Catherine Willard

All the action of the play takes place in a room in Fraulein Schneider's flat in Berlin in 1930, before the rise of the Hitler regime. The action covers about four months.

ACT I

SCENE 1: A room in Fraulein Schneider's flat in Berlin around 1930.
SCENE 2: About three months later.

ACT II

SCENE 1: Ten days later.
SCENE 2: Five days later.

ACT III

SCENE 1: Two days later.
SCENE 2: Afternoon, about three days later.
SCENE 3: Three days later. Evening.

NOTE TO PRODUCERS

"I AM A CAMERA" is based on Christopher Isherwood's short story "Sally Bowles," which appears now in his volume called *The Berlin Stories*. It has had added to it small bits from some of the other short stories in that volume, and some invention that is my own. The story of Sally Bowles appealed to me when I first read it, over fifteen years ago. I knew, then, that there was a play buried in it, but it was only recently, and through an accident, that I turned to look for it. Then I found it hidden only a few feet below the surface. I wrote the play swiftly.

It was not easy to get it put on the stage. The manuscript found many objections, quite apart from what was considered the "unpleasantness" of the character of Sally. Too many people found the play plotless, pointless and leading nowhere. I would like to take a moment to deal with these objections. That the play is plotless, at any rate in the old-fashioned sense, I agree to. But I have never been good at either inventing or writing plots, and I have done my best work always without them. And they seem to me to be growing less and less necessary in the theatre. That strikes me as one of the blessings that the movies and television have done for the stage. They have taken plot to themselves. In its place, two other things seem to have become necessary—characters and mood. Both of these, I think, the CAMERA has. Both were there in the short story, and my principal function was to transfer them to the theatre. The mood of the play—the establishment for the audience of what it felt like to be living in Berlin in 1930, and the kind of life and people that one met there, then—is its most important quality. That is what the director must aim for.

As to the play's pointlessness, the fact that it leads nowhere, and has an ending that is neither happy nor unhappy, nor of any especial promise of either for any of the characters—there, too, I must plead guilty. But I do not regard that as a fault. To finish any story, other than by death, is to lie about life. A marriage is a temporary curtain, at best, promising another play about what it was like for those two people to be married to each other. And even death, unless all the major characters are killed, as in *Hamlet*, is an ending only for the character who dies. The ones who are left alive have lives without him or her to follow out. It seems to me that the CAMERA ended when Sally left Berlin on another of her adventures, and Chris made an attempt to go back home and start really writing. I think that I foreshadowed what the rest of Sally's life would be like—that it would be like what we had seen of this section of it; and as for Christopher, I was helped there by the fact that I was using (with his permission) the name of the real author, and that his works are now well known. But the episodes of their joint lives had finished, had proved something about them as people, and that, to me, was the end of the play. At the end—the very end—Chris and Sally discover that they are deeply fond of each other, that they love each other (though not in the way that stage lovers usually find each other), but they know, too—both of them—that that love is not enough to hold them together. I think audiences know that as well, and any attempt at what has been called a happy ending, any management of a happy curtain for the pair of them, would have been recognized by anyone who cares about the theatre as completely false.

Finally, I found a management in New York that liked the script well enough to take a chance on its production. Then came the problem of casting Sally. There again, troubles showed up. It seemed obvious, at first, that what we needed was a very lovely and sexually alluring actress, and our decision that Julie Harris was the right person to play it raised some objections. Julie, talented as everyone knew her to be, had never been cast for the qualities of beauty or voluptuousness in any of the parts that she had played. Her success in the rôle was enormous.

The casting of Sally is something over which the greatest care must be taken. Physical beauty and the obvious kind of stage allure can be actually damaging. A word from Christopher Isherwood may be of value here. When we had cast Julie Harris, I was afraid of what his reaction would be, after I had gathered the general one. I wrote to him about her. His reply was that she sounded exactly right. "Sally is not an obvious tart," he wrote me. "She is a little girl who has listened to what the grown-ups had said about tarts, and who was trying to copy those things." That seems to be worth remembering. Sally, in the play, is a little different from the Sally of the story. It seemed to me that she had to be, but even though I have been accused of softening her, I have some warnings on that subject to offer to other players and directors. Sally is a little girl, that is true; she has, as one critic remarked, one foot in the nursery and one in the stews of Berlin. Both sides of her have to be shown. The nursery is marked for her by the teddy bear and the picture of the Kitten's Awakening (both inventions of my own); the other side is marked by her flagrant conversation, and her total absence of any moral values on the subject of sex. When, in Act II, Scene 1, she sees some truth in the virtues of love and fidelity, she sees them, really and truly, for the first time. Her line of "Oh, goodness, is it?" should have the flash of a sudden new realization. Its comedy is supplied by the lateness and the intensity of her discovery.

The actress playing Sally must slur neither of these sides. Sally is selfish, thoughtless, easily moved to anger and boredom. She thinks of no one else for more than a moment. She sees herself in every possible attitude, in every possible situation, and instantly starts to act it. When she thinks of becoming a nun, she really acts, for a moment, as she thinks a nun would act. That capacity for instantaneous self-dramatization is the essential thing for the actress who plays Sally.

Christopher is a difficult part. He has practically no scenes to play in which he can triumph for himself. If he tries to discover or invent them, he will find himself swinging from a chandelier that has no ceiling to depend from. His part is almost a feed part, but I can guarantee that if he will play it unselfishly, and with a true valuation of it as a commentator and observer, it will reward him very greatly. He watches Sally as an amused and no longer hungry cat would watch an impertinent mouse. He is deeply fond of her, but he is never physically attracted to her, nor does he find her romantic. It is essential to establish this in the first scene. His line of "I think you're wonderful, Sally" must be read as if it were spoken by a youngish man to a bright and impudent boy of twelve. Chris, too, is the person who moves the play from the present to the past, from the contemplative mood to the active one. This happens on the line of "I am a camera."

Natalia needs an intense seriousness in the actress. She is desperately anxious for truth and for facts, not to put other people in the wrong, but to assure herself that she is in the right. She moves from a masculine dominance to a far more submissive femininity, though her determination to stand on the truth never leaves her. But the truth about herself, and her emotional responses, shocks her when she realizes it. The actress needs to remember a masculine and formal personal carriage, German always, and she should never relax in her physical attitudes.

Fritz, too, moves from an easy self-assurance to a realization of the truth about himself and his instincts. In the first two scenes he is almost the gigolo. Then, as tragedy hits him, he becomes aware of the unpleasantness of his behavior, but he cannot handle or deal with it. He, too, has a point to go to. The last scene of Fritz and Natalia must be played as a love-scene, where the two of them are desperately moved by the mere sight of each other, and have hardly any words or moves with which to express themselves. Silences and a deep, true feeling are all that can help the actors in this scene.

Fräulein needs playing only for truth. Neither her coziness, her Rabelaisian side, her self-pity nor her Nazi affiliation should be stressed one at the expense of the other. They are all a part of her. All must be seen sharply for her to be realized.

It has been complained that Clive is an over-drawn character, and that actors who have played it have been allowed or encouraged to go too far. That I, personally, deny. Clive is a broadly-drawn character. He is, to some extent, an Englishman's idea of an American. But he is also a real person. He is a man with a neurosis, a neurosis that he is never having as good a time as he might have. He can never bear to be left alone, or to be left out of anything. Anything that he can do for someone else, so long as it includes himself as well, makes him happy. He is also, technically, of great value to the play. He breaks up the more serious moments by each of his entrances. It is essential that he be played with the greatest vitality, poise, laughter—empty, pointless laughter—and with great sweep.

The last part to be mentioned is Mrs. Watson-Courtneidge. Here I must take full responsibility, as she is a person of my own invention. She is, of course, a comedy character, and the actress must achieve this, though she must play her truthfully. There are a dozen ways to achieve the comedy for her. I see her as a woman of nerves and self-pity, using both of them to achieve her own ends. She should be played for the wish to be modern and broad-minded, and always let both attitudes slip from her just when she seems to be arriving at them. Mrs. Courtneidge is a lady, though perhaps not quite as much as she thinks she is. She has had a difficult time with her husband, and is going through another one with Sally. She is determined to be a lady always, and she aims always at the slightly genteel gesture and mannerism.

There are the parts. I know that anything that can help the mood of the show, that can produce the Berlin atmosphere of the period, is of the greatest possible help. Music—German music, played as though by a bad night-club band of those years—between the acts and scenes is of great value. All of the details of the offstage life—the funeral, the shootings, the closing of the banks—should be seen and believed in by the actors. Then the audience will believe in them, too. They are not padding. They are tremendously a part of the picture. With that, I leave the CAMERA to the new director as its film developer.

JOHN VAN DRUTEN

I AM A CAMERA

ACT I

SCENE 1

SCENE: *The scene throughout is a room in Fräulein Schneider's flat in Berlin around 1930. The bed is hidden, or partially so, behind curtains upstage* L. *The door to the hall is in the* R. *wall. Windows in the* L. *wall. The room is excessively German and middle-class. There is a tall, tiled stove with an angel on it upstage* R. *A combination washstand-cupboard like a Gothic shrine by the curtains upstage against* L. *wall. A best chair like a bishop's throne* L. *of stove. Antlers make a kind of hatstand by the door. There is a small table for tea now standing* R. *of wardrobe. The wardrobe is* C. *against rear wall, behind curtains and* L. *of bed. A backless sofa, or couch,* D. C., *and a pouffe* D. R. *of it. A large table (used as Christopher's desk)* D. L. *by the window piled with books, papers and notebooks. A chair by the table and another chair against* L. *wall, downstage of washstand. There are one or two good Medici prints on the walls, between heavy German engravings.*

TIME: *A summer afternoon.*

When the curtain rises, the stage is dark except for a light on Christopher Isherwood, seated alone at the table D. L. *He is in his twenties, English and untidy. He wears flannel trousers, very dirty, and a shirt. (He wears this throughout the play. The only change will be in his tie.) He is writing and smoking. Then he stops and reads over what he has written.*

CHRISTOPHER. (*Reading aloud.*) "In the last few days, there has been a lot of Nazi rioting in the streets, here in Berlin. They are getting bolder, more arrogant." (*He stops.*) No, that's all wrong. (*He crumples the page and throws it aside.*) That's not the right

way to start. It's sheer journalism. I must explain who it is who is telling all this—a typical beachcomber of the big city. He comes to Berlin for the week-end, stays on, runs out of money, starts giving English lessons. Now he sits in a rented room, waiting for something to happen—something that will help him understand what his life is all about. (*Rises, pouring beer into a glass, and sits on end of table.*) When Lord Tennyson wanted to write a poem, they say he used to put himself into a mystic trance by just repeating his own name. Alfred Tennyson. Christopher Isherwood. Christopher Isherwood. Christopher Isherwood. I like the sound of my name. "Alone among the writers of his generation, Christopher Isherwood can be said to have achieved true greatness." (*Drinks.*) Shut up, idiot. The only book I ever published got five reviews, all bad, and sold two hundred and thirty-three copies to date. And I haven't even started this new one, though I've been here six months already. (*Sits at the table again.*) Well, you're going to start now, this minute. You're not leaving this chair until you do. Write "Chapter One." (*Does so.*) Good. Now begin. Create something. Anything. (*He writes, then reads.*) "I am a camera, with its shutter open, quite passive. Some day all of this will have to be developed, carefully printed, fixed." (*The lights come up on the room. There is a knock on the door.*) Who's that?
SCHNEIDER. (*Off.*) It is I, Herr Issyvoo.
CHRISTOPHER. Come in, Fräulein. (*Schneider comes in, she is a large, bosomy, German woman, and carries a lace tea-cloth. She crosses to tea table* U. C. *and puts cloth down on it.*)
SCHNEIDER. I bring you this tea-cloth. When you are having a lady guest, you can trust Schneiderschen to make things elegant. (*Crosses to pouffe* D. R. *and picks up books and papers.*) Now, where do you want all of these things to go, Herr Issyvoo?
CHRISTOPHER. Oh, put them on the floor.
SCHNEIDER. But you cannot put things on the floor. (*Crosses up to behind couch.*)
CHRISTOPHER. There are a lot of things there already.
SCHNEIDER. But they must not stay there, not if a lady is coming. It does not look good at all. (*Picks up pile of laundry from couch.*)
CHRISTOPHER. You'd better put them on the bed. She won't be looking at the bed.

SCHNEIDER. And how do you know that, Herr Issyvoo? A handsome man like you? (*Moves to* L. *end of couch.*)
CHRISTOPHER. Fräulein Schneider. I'm surprised at you.
SCHNEIDER. (*With a big laugh.*) Oh, Herr Issyvoo. I have been young, too. Young and saucy. (*Rather archly, she takes the things to the bed behind the curtains.*)
CHRISTOPHER. I suppose you had a great many admirers, Fräulein Schneider? (*Picks up books from couch. During this speech Schneider crosses to couch, picks up towel and hangs it on rail* D. S. *of washstand, then returns to* R. *of Christopher.*)
SCHNEIDER. Oh, I had dozens, Herr Issyvoo. (*Christopher picks up magazines on floor and puts them on table.*) But only one friend. (*She returns for more stuff.*) Eleven years we were together. Then he died. And it was after that that I became fat. The bosom, you know. It grew and it grew. And it is such a weight to carry about with you. It is like carrying a suitcase. *Two* suitcases. (*Crosses to below couch, picks up dressing gown and slippers, then to chair* U. R. *for pyjamas, all of which she puts into wardrobe. Christopher rises.*) And it is sad that it should all have grown after he died. He was a man for bosoms. It would have made him so happy. And now it does no one any good. This young lady you are expecting: she is very attractive? (*Crosses to bed and closes curtains.*)
CHRISTOPHER. She is one of my pupils. She wanted to see where I lived. Though when I say she is one of my pupils, it isn't true. She's the only one I have left. The others have all gone away for the summer. (*Turns and steps to her.*) Fräulein Schneider, I have got to have a talk with you.
SCHNEIDER. Ja, Herr Issyvoo?
CHRISTOPHER. I don't think I can go on living here.
SCHNEIDER. What? Oh, Herr Issyvoo, you are not going to leave me? Are you not comfortable here?
CHRISTOPHER. Yes, I am very comfortable here. It's just that I can't afford it.
SCHNEIDER. Oh, that can wait.
CHRISTOPHER. No. It's been waiting too long. I haven't paid you for two months, not properly. I've got it here. (*Takes money from wallet.*) I was just wondering: that little room across the passage, just across the passage, that's not let?
SCHNEIDER. But it is so small, Herr Issyvoo. Why, you could

hardly get into it. And what do I do with this room? With the summer coming on, I shall never find a tenant for it.
CHRISTOPHER. (*Handing her money.*) Oh, I'm sure you will.
SCHNEIDER. Danke.
CHRISTOPHER. And until you do, why don't you live in it yourself, instead of the sitting-room?
SCHNEIDER. (*Bringing table to* U. L. *of couch and setting tea-cloth.*) I like the sitting-room. (*Christopher sits* C. *of couch.*) I can look on to the corner and see what's going on. And believe me, Herr Issyvoo, there is plenty. Those women, they are as old as I am—almost—and they stand there and whisper to all the men who pass by: Komm, Süsser. And believe me, Herr Issyvoo, they come. (*Moves round to front of table.*) Sometimes I think I shall adopt that profession myself.
CHRISTOPHER. Can I rent the other room, Fräulein Schneider? What do you charge for it?
SCHNEIDER. (*Crossing to above couch,* L. *of Christopher.*) I have charged twenty-eight marks when times were good.
CHRISTOPHER. I can't afford twenty-eight.
SCHNEIDER. (*Ruffling his hair.*) Ach, du armer Junger. But of course you can rent it. I will not have you leave. You rent it for twenty marks.
CHRISTOPHER. You're very sweet, Fräulein Schneider.
SCHNEIDER. Sweet? Ja. Once I was sweet. Sweet as a sugar cake. Now I am sweet like a fat old bun. (*Crosses to table and tidies it.*) And soon you make a great deal of money with your stories that you are always writing, and you take this room again, and everyone is happy once more.
CHRISTOPHER. I'll buy you a fur coat.
SCHNEIDER. Ja! And then I become one of the ladies. Only I will not go up and down the street in those high heels. I sit at my window in my fur coat and call out, "Komm, Süsser." Komm to the third floor. And then I open the coat a little, just a little, and what do you think I have on underneath? Nothing! I have nothing on underneath. (*Bell rings.*) Ach Gott, there is the bell. It will be your young lady. (*Takes beer bottle, glass and plate from table and crosses to door.*)
CHRISTOPHER. You need not tell her that I am leaving this room.
SCHNEIDER. (*On her way out.*) But of course not, Herr Issyvoo.

You can trust me perfectly. (*Turns to him.*) And I will bring you paper serviettes for your coffee. Most ladylike. Ladies appreciate these things. (*Goes out, leaving door open. Christopher crosses to washstand and straightens his tie.*)

FRITZ. (*Off.*) Herr Issyvoo?

SCHNEIDER. (*Off.*) Nein, nein, Herr Wendel. Sie können nicht hinein gehen. Herr Issyvoo erwartet heute eine Dame.

FRITZ. (*Off.*) Aber ich muss mit ihm sprechen. Christopher. Christopher.

CHRISTOPHER. (*Going to door.*) Fritz. (*Fritz enters, young and dark.*)

FRITZ. (*At door.*) Fräulein Schneider says I cannot come in. She says you expect a lady.

CHRISTOPHER. Yes, I do. But that's all right. Come in, Fritz. (*Schneider stands behind.*) Do you want some coffee? One of my pupils is coming.

FRITZ. But yes, I would like some coffee. *Black* coffee.

CHRISTOPHER. Will you make enough for three, Fräulein Schneider?

SCHNEIDER. You are too good, Herr Issyvoo. You entertain whoever comes. No matter whoever. (*Goes out, shutting door. Christopher takes Fritz's hat and cane. He bangs hat on hatstand and puts cane in umbrella stand.*)

FRITZ. (*Crosses in front of couch to* L. *of it, taking gloves off.*) I do not think your landlady likes me. And that is with me all right. Ultimately, I do not like her, too. In fact, I think the world is lousy.

CHRISTOPHER. Is business bad? (*Coming down to* R. *of Fritz and offering cigarette which he refuses.*)

FRITZ. It is terrible. Lousy and terrible. Or I pull off a new deal in the next month, or I go as a gigolo.

CHRISTOPHER. (*Sits* R. *end of couch and lights cigarette.*) Either—or. I'm sorry. That's just force of habit.

FRITZ. I am speaking a lousy English just now. Sally says maybe she will give me a few lessons.

CHRISTOPHER. Who is Sally?

FRITZ. (*Crossing above couch to* L. *of Christopher.*) She is a friend of mine. Eventually she is coming around here this afternoon. I want that you should know each other.

CHRISTOPHER. Is she a girl friend of yours?

FRITZ. Not yet. But she is wonderful, Chris.
CHRISTOPHER. Who is she? What does she do?
FRITZ. She is an actress. She sings at the Lady Windermere. Hot stuff, believe me. Ultimately she has a bit of French in her. Her mother was French. (*Crosses to hatstand and puts gloves with hat.*)
CHRISTOPHER. I wonder what Natalia will think of her. Natalia Landauer is the pupil I am expecting.
FRITZ. (*Crosses to above* R. *end of couch.*) Landauer? Of the big department store?
CHRISTOPHER. Her father owns it. It's the family business.
FRITZ. But they must be enormously wealthy.
CHRISTOPHER. Oh, yes, they're stinking rich.
FRITZ. (*Kneeling on side arm of couch.*) And are you going to marry her?
CHRISTOPHER. (*Laughing.*) Me? No, of course not.
FRITZ. Do you not want her?
CHRISTOPHER. Not a bit. Except as a pupil.
FRITZ. Then if I should meet her and perhaps make a pass after her, you would not mind?
CHRISTOPHER. But you haven't even seen her.
FRITZ. (*Moving across to table* L.) Why would that make a difference? I tell you, Chris, I need money. Maybe then her father will take a liking from me, and give me a job in the business. If I marry her, a partnership perhaps.
CHRISTOPHER. What makes you think she'd have you?
FRITZ. All women will have me if I want them.
CHRISTOPHER. Not Sally, apparently.
FRITZ. (*Crosses below couch to pouffe* D. R. *and sits.*) Sally has been too busy. With other men. But one day she will be free, and then I will ultimately get my look in.
CHRISTOPHER. (*Teasing him.*) Perhaps *you* won't be free. Perhaps you will be all tied up with Natalia.
FRITZ. (*Seriously.*) Yes, ultimately business must come first. I suppose she is a Jewess?
CHRISTOPHER. Oh, yes.
FRITZ. Well, there is always something. And you know, Chris, I am very broad-minded. (*Bell rings.*)
CHRISTOPHER. (*Rising.*) That will be Natalia.
FRITZ. (*Rising and moving up to* R. *of couch.*) How do I look,

Chris? How is my hair? (*Gets out a comb and mirror.*) Um Gotteswillen . . . a grey hair. No, that is too much. (*Pulls it out.*) You see, Chris dear, I must marry soon. You will help me to arrange the marriage settlement? (*They meet in front of couch. Voices off.*)

SALLY. (*Off.*) Herr Isherwood ist er zu Hause?

FRITZ. That is Sally. Chris, put on your coat.

CHRISTOPHER. Why?

FRITZ. She is a lady. Very elegant. (*Christopher crosses to chair above desk for his coat.*)

SCHNEIDER. (*Off.*) He is not here. He is not to house.

SALLY. (*Off.*) But he must be. He is expecting me. Isn't Herr Wendel here?

FRITZ. (*Going to the door while Christopher puts his coat on.*) Sally—liebling . . . (*Exit.*)

SALLY. (*Off.*) Fritz, darling. The old lady said there was nobody here.

FRITZ. Come in. (*Sally comes in with Fritz behind her. She is young and attractive. She wears black silk with a small cape over her shoulders, and a page boy's cap stuck jauntily on one side of her head. Her finger-nails are painted emerald green. Schneider stands again in the doorway.*) Sally, this is Christopher. Christopher, this is Sally. Sally Bowles. (*Christopher and Sally meet in front of couch* C.)

CHRISTOPHER. How do you do?

SALLY. (*Shaking hands.*) I'm terribly glad to meet you.

CHRISTOPHER. Make coffee for four, will you, Fräulein Schneider?

SALLY. Oh, not for me. I'm allergic to coffee. I come out in the most sinister spots if I drink it before dinner.

CHRISTOPHER. (*To Schneider.*) Just for three, then. (*Schneider goes, shutting the door.*)

SALLY. I always have Prairie Oysters for breakfast. Don't you adore them? Eggs with Worcester Sauce all sort of wooshed up together. I simply live on them. (*Sits, draping cloak over head of couch.*) Actually, I suppose I couldn't have a whisky and soda, could I? I'm simply dead.

CHRISTOPHER. I'm afraid I haven't got any whisky.

SALLY. I thought you were English.

CHRISTOPHER. I am. But I'm also poor.

SALLY. Oh, so am I. Terribly poor. But I always have whisky. I mean, I think one must. Do you have anything? I mean, anything besides coffee?
CHRISTOPHER. I think I've got a little spot of gin.
SALLY. Dear old mother's ruin. Gin will be wonderful. (*Christopher gets gin out of cupboard.*) Am I terribly late, Fritz darling?
FRITZ. (*Leaning over head of couch.*) No, you are beautifully on time.
SALLY. I thought I wasn't going to be able to come at all. I had a most frantic row with my landlady. Finally, I just said pig, and swept out. (*Moving down to* L. *of couch.*)
CHRISTOPHER. What would you like in this—or this in?
SALLY. Have you got anything?
CHRISTOPHER. (*Helplessly.*) No, I don't think I have.
SALLY. Then I'll just have it straight.
CHRISTOPHER. (*Going back to cupboard.*) I'm afraid it will have to be in a tooth glass.
SALLY. That will be wonderful. Give me one of your marvellous cigarettes, Fritz darling. (*Fritz offers cigarettes.*) Do you ever smoke any of Fritz's cigarettes? (*Takes holder from her handbag, fits cigarette into it and lights it.*) They're absolutely devastating. I'm sure they're full of opium, or something. They always make me feel terribly sensual.
CHRISTOPHER. (*Handing her the glass.*) Here you are. (*Leaves gin bottle on the tea table.*)
SALLY. Thank you so much. This looks wonderful. (*Sips it.*) Oh, it is. It's got an extraordinary taste, like peppermint.
CHRISTOPHER. Oh, I'm afraid I can't have washed out this glass properly. That must be toothpaste. I'm so sorry.
SALLY. I think it is wonderful. Have some, Fritz. (*Hands Fritz the glass.*) Taste it. Perhaps we can all make a fortune selling mint-flavored gin.
FRITZ. (*Tasting.*) It is extremely interesting. (*Hands glass back to Sally.*)
SALLY. (*Handing glass to Christopher.*) You have some, too.
CHRISTOPHER. (*Tasting.*) Perhaps we can all make a fortune selling mouthwash you can get drunk on. (*Moves away to table* L. *and sits on* R. *edge.*)
FRITZ. (*Sitting on head of couch.*) What for was your row with your landlady?

SALLY. Oh, it was absolutely awful. You should have heard the things she called me. I mean—well, I suppose in a way I may be a bit of a tart . . . I mean, in a nice way—but one doesn't like to be called that. Just because I brought a man home with me last night. And, anyway, I'm terribly in love with him.
FRITZ. Anyone I know?
SALLY. You'll never guess. Klaus.
FRITZ. (*Rising and leaning over Sally.*) Klaus? Your accompanist, Klaus?
SALLY. Yes. He was always just like part of the piano to me. And then last night he was absolutely astonishing. Just like a faun, or something. He made me feel like a most marvellous nymph, miles away from anywhere, in the middle of the forest. And then the landlady came in and made the most boring remarks, so I simply can't go back. (*Finishes drink and hands glass to Fritz, who returns it to the cupboard.*) I shall have to find a new room. (*To Christopher.*) I don't suppose you know of any, do you?
CHRISTOPHER. (*Rises and moves in to* L. *of couch.*) A room?
SALLY. Something like this, perhaps?
CHRISTOPHER. Well, there is this one.
FRITZ. (*Moving down to* L. *of Christopher.*) Why, are you leaving?
CHRISTOPHER. I'm leaving this room. I can't afford it any more.
SALLY. Is it terribly expensive? (*Fritz moves chair from above table to* R. *of it and sits facing them.*)
CHRISTOPHER. I pay fifty marks a month. That includes breakfast.
SALLY. (*Rising. Christopher follows her round to above couch.*) But that's nothing. I pay eighty for mine. This is very nice. (*Looks around.*) Is that your bed? Oh, I think that's sweet—all hidden away like that. (*Looks behind the curtains.*) Oh, that's where you keep things.
CHRISTOPHER. (*Laughing.*) Only when I have visitors.
SALLY. You mean I could really have this? How soon?
CHRISTOPHER. As soon as you like. I've only got to move across the hall. It won't take me a minute. And I know Fräulein Schneider is very anxious to let it.
SALLY. (*Coming down to* L. *of Christopher.*) What is she like? I mean, is she going to make trouble if I bring men home occasionally? I mean, it would only be very occasionally, because I

do think one ought to go to the man's rooms, if one can. I mean, it doesn't look so much as if one was sort of expecting it. (*Kneels on couch.*) And men feel very keenly about that sort of thing. And it won't be men, anyway. It'll only be Klaus. I've decided to be absolutely faithful to him. I really have. She wouldn't mind that, would she, or would she?

CHRISTOPHER. If she can let the room, I'm sure she wouldn't mind anything.

SALLY. I say, am I shocking you, talking like this?

CHRISTOPHER. Not a bit. No one ever shocks me when they try to.

SALLY. (*Rather sharply.*) Why do you say I'm trying to shock you?

CHRISTOPHER. I have an idea you like to try and shock everyone. Why do you paint your finger-nails green?

SALLY. I think it's pretty. Don't you?

CHRISTOPHER. Suppose you thought it was pretty to paint dirty pictures on them, would you do that, too?

SALLY. Yes. You know, that's rather a good idea. Not dirty pictures exactly, but sort of *stimulating* ones. I must get someone to do it for me. Is he really unshockable, Fritz, or is he just pretending?

FRITZ. Oh, no, Chris is quite unshockable. I have tried many times, but ultimately I cannot do it.

CHRISTOPHER. But—there is a young lady coming this afternoon who *is* shockable. So would you mind awfully being just a bit more careful what you say? She's one of my pupils, and I do rather need her.

SALLY. Oh, but darling, of course. I'll be terribly ladylike.

CHRISTOPHER. And don't let her know I'm going to move out of here; do you mind? I don't want her to know how broke I am!

SALLY. I won't breathe a word. (*Bell rings. Fritz moves* U. C.)

CHRISTOPHER. (*Starting to go to door.*) That must be her now.

SALLY. You'd better put the gin away.

CHRISTOPHER. Oh, yes, thanks. (*Retrieves gin from tea table and puts it in cupboard.*)

SALLY. I'm afraid there isn't time for me to clean my nails. I'll try and keep my fists clenched. (*Christopher crosses to door.*)

NATALIA. (*Off.*) Herr Isherwood?

SCHNEIDER. Ja, gnädiges Fräulein. Er erwartet Sie. Bitte sehr. (*The door opens and Schneider ushers in Natalia.*)
SCHNEIDER. Bitte. Hier ist die Dame die sie erwartet haben, Herr Issyvoo. (*Exit. Natalia is about twenty-two, correctly dressed, very German, formal and decided. Christopher leads her to* C. *below couch.*)
CHRISTOPHER. Natalia. These are friends of mine. Miss Bowles, Fräulein Landauer, and Mr. Wendel, Fräulein Landauer.
FRITZ. (*Moving round to* R. *of Natalia clicks his heels and bows. Natalia bows to him.*) Sehr erfreut, gnädiges, Fräulein.
CHRISTOPHER. I think we'd better speak English. Fraulein Landauer speaks wonderful English.
FRITZ. I am charmed, dearest Miss. (*Clicks heels and bows. Natalia bows again, then shakes hands with Sally, noticing her nails.*)
SALLY. (*Concealing her nails.*) How do you do? (*Sitting on chair* R. *of desk. Fritz crosses to pouffe and sits. Christopher sits on head of couch.*)
NATALIA. (*Sitting on* L. *end of couch.*) I am well. I have just had a cold, but it is better now.
SALLY. (*Doing her best.*) Oh, I'm so sorry. Colds are beastly things, aren't they? One's head gets all stopped up.
NATALIA. This was a cold in the chest. It was not in my head. All the *plegm* was here. (*Points to her chest.*)
SALLY. All the what?
NATALIA. The *plegm* that comes into the tubes.
CHRISTOPHER. Phlegm. You pronounce the "h."
NATALIA. Oh. Then why do you say phthisis, what the Lady of the Camellias had, and not pronounce the "h" there, too? (*A pause while she waits for an answer.*)
CHRISTOPHER. Well . . .
NATALIA. There must be a reason. You give it to me, please.
CHRISTOPHER. I don't know it. But you don't say p-tisis, either.
NATALIA. Then you should say "lem," and leave it right out as in phthisis. I have lem in my chest. Is it not so? It is not an exact language, your English. (*Takes gloves off.*)
SALLY. What *is* phthisis?
NATALIA. It is consumption. From the lungs. They are consumed in phlegm.
SALLY. Do you mind not going on about it? I think I am going

to be sick. (*Schneider enters with the coffee tray and places it on tea table. She goes out, leaving door open.*)
NATALIA. But why should it make you sick? You do not have it.
SALLY. All stories about illness make me want to throw up. I saw a film about syphilis the other night that was too awful. I couldn't let a man touch me for almost a week. Is it true you can get it from kissing?
FRITZ. Oh, yes. And your King, Henry the Eighth, caught it from letting Cardinal Wolsey whisper to him.
NATALIA. That is not, I think, founded in fact. But kissing, most decidedly yes. And from towels. And cups. I hope these have been cleaned properly.
CHRISTOPHER. (*Flippantly.*) Oh, yes, Fräulein Schneider always boils them every day. (*Schneider re-enters with cake stand and puts it down,* R. *of tea table.*)
SALLY. I mean, you can't ask every man to run out and have tests and things before you let him touch you. I mean, there isn't time, and he'd be off in a nip to someone far less particular. (*Schneider crosses to above couch. Natalia freezes. Christopher comes in hastily.*)
CHRISTOPHER. (*Crossing to tea table.*) Natalia, let me give you some coffee.
SALLY. (*Rising.*) Oh, Fräulein. (*Crosses to Schneider.*) Could I have a talk with your landlady, Chris, darling?
CHRISTOPHER. There's plenty of time.
SALLY. Oh, we'll talk outside. Won't we, Fräulein darling? We'll have secrets together. (*To Natalia.*) If you'll excuse me.
NATALIA. But most obligingly.
SALLY. (*To Schneider.*) Komm, liebes Fraulein, wir werden haben Geheimnesse zusammen. (*Exit with Schneider. Fritz rises and crosses to cake stand. Takes plate and hands it to Natalia.*)
FRITZ. (*To Natalia, while Christopher passes coffee.*) You will allow me to pass you a cake, dearest Miss? They are jam tarts.
NATALIA. I thank you, no. I do not eat between meals. (*Fritz puts plate back.*) And Miss is not the correct way to address a lady in English. No sugar, neither. Just plain black coffee.
FRITZ. (*Moves round to* U. R. *of Natalia and offers cigarette, which she takes.*) That, too, is how *I* like it. Black, black, black, like Otello.

NATALIA. You tell me, please, about Fräulein Bowles. She is a remarkable girl.
FRITZ. (*Lighting her cigarette.*) She is a night-club artiste. Very talented. (*Christopher hands coffee to Natalia and returns to tea table.*)
NATALIA. Where does she perform?
FRITZ. (*Sits on side arm of couch.*) At a club calling the Lady Windermere. You know perhaps the play from Oscar Villder, calling *Lady Windermere's Fan*? (*Fritz crosses to table for ashtray, collects coffee from Christopher and returns to head of couch, putting ashtray down on couch on the way.*)
NATALIA. (*Correcting him.*) Called *Lady Windermere's Fan* by Oscar Vilt. But of course I know it. I have read it, both in English and in German. I think it is better in German. But the club I do not know.
FRITZ. Would you let me take you to it one night, to hear Sally sing?
CHRISTOPHER. (*Sitting on chair* R. *of desk.*) Do you think it is quite the right place for Fräulein Landauer? (*Fritz sits on pouffe.*)
NATALIA. But why not?
CHRISTOPHER. Oh, I don't know. I just thought . . .
NATALIA. You thought what, please?
CHRISTOPHER. I don't know, really.
NATALIA. You don't know. Then I cannot help you.
CHRISTOPHER. I thought it might be just a bit—Bohemian.
NATALIA. Then I must see it. I accept your invitation, my dear sir. When shall we go?
FRITZ. (*Rising and moving in to Natalia.*) We could go tonight, if you are free.
NATALIA. I can be free. I will give you my address. (*Hands Fritz a visiting card.*) You will come, too, Christopher, and we will be a party to hear your girl friend sing.
CHRISTOPHER. She is not my girl friend.
NATALIA. No? Then what is she, please?
CHRISTOPHER. She's—just a friend.
NATALIA. I see. And she is not a girl?
CHRISTOPHER. Yes, but . . .
NATALIA. Then why is she not a girl friend?
FRITZ. Girl friend means something more than a friend who is a girl, Fräulein.

NATALIA. So? What does it mean?
FRITZ. It means a sweetheart.
NATALIA. Ah, so I did not know. Then I am not a girl friend of yours, Christopher?
CHRISTOPHER. (*Feebly.*) Unfortunately—no . . .
NATALIA. You do not mean that, Christopher. You say it only to be polite.
FRITZ. He ought to mean it.
NATALIA. (*Ever so slightly coquettish.*) You think, Herr Wendel?
FRITZ. I think very much.
NATALIA. And you, too, are polite. (*Puts cigarette out.*)
FRITZ. No, I am never polite. I am only sincere. (*Returns ashtray to table. Sally re-enters, smoking.*)
SALLY. It's all fixed up, Chris. The poor old thing was almost in tears of gratitude. (*Sits* R. *of Natalia.*)
NATALIA. And why was she so grateful?
SALLY. Because I'm moving in here. (*Fritz puts cup down on tea table.*)
CHRISTOPHER. (*Rises and crosses to* R. *of couch. Hurriedly.*) Sally! We are all coming to hear you sing tonight.
SALLY. Tonight? Oh, but, my dear, I shall be exhausted. I didn't sleep a wink last night. (*Christopher sits on pouffe.*)
NATALIA. You had rather I come some other evening?
SALLY. Oh, I expect it will be all right. Only don't let the proprietor bother you. He's quite a darling, really, but he takes dope quite a lot, and sometimes it doesn't agree with him. (*Puts cigarette out in Natalia's cup.*) He pinches people. It doesn't mean anything.
NATALIA. (*Stiffly.*) I think now that I must go. (*Rises and hands cup to Fritz.*)
FRITZ. Please, if I may accompany you?
NATALIA. My dear young man, I am not sixty years old, and I can go home unmolested all by myself. (*Fritz puts cup down on tea table.*)
CHRISTOPHER. (*Quoting.*) Bin weder Fräulein, weder schön, kann ungeleitet nach Hause gehen.
SALLY. What is that?
NATALIA. (*Reverently.*) It is from *Faust*

CHRISTOPHER. It means, "I am not a virgin, and I am not beautiful, and I can go home alone."

FRITZ. (*Moving down to below Natalia. Earnestly.*) Oh, but that is not true. None of it is true. Not in this case.

SALLY. (*Eagerly.*) You mean you think Fräulein Landauer *is* a virgin? How do you know?

NATALIA. You are filled with interesting curiosity, Fräulein Bowles, but I must pull myself away. I say good-bye. (*Shakes hands with Sally. Fritz collects hat, cane, etc.*)

SALLY. Good-bye.

NATALIA. Good-bye, Christopher. (*Shakes hands.*) I think I will talk to your landlady on my way out. I do not like these rooms, and she is charging you too much. (*Exit with Fritz. Sally lies back on couch.*)

SALLY. (*After a moment.*) I don't think that girl liked me very much, did she?

CHRISTOPHER. (*Crossing to tea table for cake and napkin.*) No, I don't think she really did.

SALLY. I'm sure I don't know why, I was doing my best. It won't make any difference to you, will it? To your lessons, I mean?

CHRISTOPHER. (*Moves down to chair* R. *of table* L.) No, I don't think so. She's very broad-minded in an intellectual sort of way. She'll probably decide it's her duty to understand you.

SALLY. What on earth was Fritz up to? I can't think what got into him. He isn't after her, is he?

CHRISTOPHER. She's very rich, you know. And Fritz is very broke.

SALLY. Do you think he'll get anywhere with her?

CHRISTOPHER. (*Sits.*) I've always understood from him that women find him attractive.

SALLY. (*Taking cigarette from handbag.*) I shouldn't think *she* would, with his going on like that. I should think his best way with a girl of that kind would be to make a pounce.

CHRISTOPHER. I can't imagine anyone pouncing on Natalia.

SALLY. (*Lighting cigarette.*) No, dear. That's why it would be so effective.

CHRISTOPHER. I believe you're right. You know, that's quite wonderful of you, Sally.

SALLY. It seems very simple to me. Give me the rest of that gin,

will you, Chris? There's just a little left. Then you won't have to pack the bottle.
CHRISTOPHER. (*Getting it.*) Of course.
SALLY. And you're going to be right across the hall. I took a look at the room. It's not very nice. But you can use this any time you like, you know, and then if I'm low—or you are (*Rises.*) we can just sob on each other's bosoms. (*Sally and Christopher meet in front of couch. He gives her drink.*) I say, Fräulein Schneider's got a big one, hasn't she? Like an opera singer, or that woman in the music halls who can make hers jump. (*Crossing to table* L.) Can Fräulein Schneider do that?
CHRISTOPHER. We might train her.
SALLY. (*Looking at the paper on the table.*) Chapter One. Are you writing a novel?
CHRISTOPHER. Starting one. (*Moves across to* R. *end of couch and sits lighting cigarette.*)
SALLY. (*Reading.*) "I am a Camera, with its shutter open, quite passive." Do you mean this is a story written by a camera?
CHRISTOPHER. (*Laughing.*) No, it's written by me. I'm the camera.
SALLY. How do you mean?
CHRISTOPHER. I'm the one who sees it all. I don't take part. I don't really even think. I just sort of photograph it. Ask questions, maybe. How long have you been in Germany?
SALLY. About two months.
CHRISTOPHER. What part of England is your home in?
SALLY. Lancashire, my father owns a mill—several mills!
CHRISTOPHER. And your mother is French. (*She looks blank.*) Fritz told me she was.
SALLY. (*Puts cigarette out and crosses to* R. *end of couch. Irritated.*) Fritz is an idiot. He's always inventing things. Mummy's a bit county, but she's an absolute darling. I simply worship her. I'm afraid Daddy's side of the family comes out in me. You'd love Daddy. He doesn't care a damn for anyone. It was he who said I could go to London and learn acting. You see, I couldn't bear school, so I got myself expelled.
CHRISTOPHER. How did you do that?
SALLY. I told the headmistress I was going to have a baby.
CHRISTOPHER. Oh, rot, Sally, you didn't.
SALLY. Yes, I did. So they got a doctor to examine me, and then

when they found out there was nothing the matter they were most frightfully disappointed. And the headmistress said that a girl who could even think of anything so disgusting couldn't possibly be let stay on. So I went to London. (*Crosses to pouffe and sits.*) And that's where things started happening.

CHRISTOPHER. What sort of things?

SALLY. Oh—things. I had a wonderful, voluptuous little room—with no chairs—(*Drinks.*) that's how I used to seduce men. One of them told me I'd do better in Berlin. What do you think, Chris?

CHRISTOPHER. I think you're doing fine. (*Sits on floor in front of couch.*) I think you're wonderful, Sally.

SALLY. Do you, Chris dear? I think you're wonderful, too. We're going to be real good friends, aren't we?

CHRISTOPHER. (*Rather slowly.*) Do you know, I believe we are. Real good friends.

SALLY. (*Rising and walking behind couch.*) You know, Chris, you were quite right about my wanting to shock people. I do, and I don't know why. (*Puts glass down on tea table.*) I do think you were clever to notice it. (*Picks up paper knife from desk and plays with it.*) And, Chris, there's one thing more. I'm not sure if you'll understand or not. I did tell Fritz my mother was French. I suppose I wanted to impress him.

CHRISTOPHER. What's so impressive about a French mother?

SALLY. I suppose it's like tarts calling themselves French names to excite men. I'm a bit mad like that sometimes, Chris. You must be patient with me.

CHRISTOPHER. I will, Sally. Was that all true just now, what you told me about your family?

SALLY. Yes, of course it was. (*Moves round to* R. *of desk.*) Well, most of it. (*Puts paper knife down.*) Only, Chris, you mustn't ever ask me questions. If I want to tell you anything, I will. But I've got to be free.

CHRISTOPHER. (*Amused.*) Very well, Sally. (*Rises.*)

SALLY. I've got to have a free soul. You know, I think I'm really rather a strange and extraordinary person, Chris.

CHRISTOPHER. So do I, Sally. (*Copying her tone.*) Quite extraordinary. (*Christopher starts to laugh. Sally joins in. Their laughter grows louder. She embraces him.*)

SALLY. Oh, Chris, you are awful. (*Releasing herself, she picks up her handbag and starts for the door.*) Look, darling, I must go.

I'll be back in an hour with all my things, and you can help me unpack. So long, Chris. (*Exit.*)
CHRISTOPHER. (*Following her to door.*) So long, Sally. (*During this speech Christopher moves paper knife from couch to table* L., *puts gin bottle in waste-paper basket and replaces chair above table.*) Well, I'd better start moving out of here. I bet Fräulein Schneider's pleased. Sally is just the kind of person she likes. (*Takes two personal pictures from the wall and puts them on the table.*) How do I know that? How do I know what kind of a person Sally is? I suppose that's what's so fascinating about her. People who talk like that about themselves *ought* to be lying. But I don't believe she is. And yet she's that mysterious thing my family calls a lady, too. (*Looks out of the window.*) Look at her. She's even flirting with the taxi-driver. And she knows I'm watching her. Oh, my God! (*He laughs.*) I've got to put that down right away. (*Sits at the desk and starts to write in a notebook.*) Let's make notes. How would you describe her? Sally Bowles was a girl of about . . . I wonder how old she is. Her face is young, but her hands look terribly old. And they were dirty, too. Dirty as a little girl's hands. (*Writes again.*) Sally's hands were like the old hands of a dirty little girl.

CURTAIN

ACT I

SCENE 2

About three months later.
The scene is very slightly changed. A few feminine touches. A doll or two. Some bottles and jars are spread out on the table. The Medici prints are missing, and a couple of other pictures, very sentimental, are in their places. A pair of silk stockings and a pair of panties on a hanger, drying. When the curtain rises Schneider is tidying up the table L. *There is a knock on the door.*

SCHNEIDER. Ja, herein. (*Christopher enters and moves* U. R. *to tea table.*)
CHRISTOPHER. Oh, is Sally not here?

SCHNEIDER. No, Herr, Issyvoo, she has gone out. And so late she was getting up. It's not as if she were working nights any more. I don't think she is well, Herr Issyvoo.
CHRISTOPHER. Do you know where she keeps my thermometer, Fräulein Schneider? I want to take my temperature. (*Moves down to* L. *of couch.*)
SCHNEIDER. What, again?
CHRISTOPHER. I've got pains in my back, strange pains.
SCHNEIDER. (*Moving in to Christopher.*) I thought it was your stomach.
CHRISTOPHER. That was yesterday. (*Moves towards Schneider and they meet between couch and table* L.)
SCHNEIDER. (*Feeling his head.*) You have no temperature.
CHRISTOPHER. (*Sitting on couch.*) I'm not so sure. I'd like to see, if I can find the thermometer.
SCHNEIDER. (*Looking for it.*) It must be here somewhere. I saw her using it only yesterday to stir those Prairie Oysters with. Ah, here it is. There is still a little egg on it, but it's on the case. (*Finds thermometer under doll on tea table, gives it to Christopher and puts case on washstand.*)
CHRISTOPHER. Thank you. (*Opens thermometer and shakes it down.*) Has the afternoon post come yet?
SCHNEIDER. (*Moves round to head of couch and picks up a slip and pair of stockings.*) It will be here soon, now. There was nothing for her this morning. (*Christopher puts the thermometer in his mouth.*) I begin to worry for Fräulein Sally. That friend Klaus of hers. Six weeks he has been away now in England and only one letter has he written. (*Bell rings.*) There is the bell. (*She goes to answer it.*)
FRITZ. (*Off.*) Ist Fräulein Bowles zu Hause?
SCHNEIDER. (*Off.*) Nein, Herr Wendel. Aber Herr Issyvoo ist da. In ihren Zimmer. Gehen nur hinein. (*Fritz enters.*)
FRITZ. Hello, Chris. Are you ill?
CHRISTOPHER. I don't know yet. Sit down.
FRITZ. (*Sitting* R. *of Christopher.*) What's the matter?
CHRISTOPHER. My back aches. That could be the beginning of paralysis—creeping paralysis. Fritz, read this for me.
FRITZ. (*Takes thermometer.*) It is ninety-eight point six. Um Gotteswillen! but of that a man is dead.
CHRISTOPHER. (*Takes thermometer from him.*) No, you are

mixing it up with Centigrade. You don't die Fahrenheit until it's over one hundred and six. Are you sure that's what it says?
FRITZ. Quite sure.
CHRISTOPHER. (*Removing the thermometer.*) It must be broken. (*Shakes thermometer down.*) I think I'll take some aspirin. (*Crosses up to washstand, puts thermometer down and takes aspirin from cupboard.*) How are you, Fritz? How's Natalia?
FRITZ. Christopher. I cannot get anywhere with that girl. I have spent money on her. Money I have not got. I meet her parents. I write her poems. Poems from Heinrich Heine, and always she recognizes them, and then she laughs at me. It is not even the money any more. (*Crosses to table* L. *and sits on edge.*) But when she will not let me make love to her, it drives me ultimately mad. I kiss her, and it is like my aunt. And, Chris, she is beautiful, and she is untouched. By me or anybody.
CHRISTOPHER. (*Swallowing aspirin.*) Sally said you ought to pounce on her.
FRITZ. But no one could pounce on Natalia.
CHRISTOPHER. (*Crosses to couch and lies down on it, picking up teddy bear.*) Sally said that's why it would be so effective. Knock her down. Throw her on a couch or something.
FRITZ. You do not mean that, Chris.
CHRISTOPHER. You don't seem to be doing any good the usual way. How do you ordinarily manage with women?
FRITZ. I have only to uncurl my little finger, and purr a little, and they come running. I think perhaps I try. (*Rises and crosses to above* L. *of Christopher.*) I can after all do myself no harm. She is away now. I write to her every day. Now I will write no more. I wait for her to come home, and then I will pounce, and I will snarl.
CHRISTOPHER. Good.
FRITZ. And what is with you, Chris? You still live in that dark tiny prison of a room?
CHRISTOPHER. Oh, yes.
FRITZ. And can you get anyone else in the room at the same time?
CHRISTOPHER. Oh, yes. If they're fond of me.
FRITZ. (*Leaning over him.*) Do you have any love-life now?
CHRISTOPHER. I have a little. Now and then.
FRITZ. And you will not talk about it. Not ever. You English are

so *reticent.* (*Crosses* U. L. *to "Kitten's Awakening" picture.*) If Sally did not ultimately have a French mother, she would not talk about it, either.
CHRISTOPHER. A what? (*Remembering.*) Oh . . . yes.
FRITZ. She is a strange girl. Half of her is so ultimately frank, and half is so sentimental. (*Takes a picture from the wall.*) This picture. She has it with her everywhere. (*Comes back to above* L. *of Christopher.*) It is called "The Kitten's Awakening." It is childish. (*Sally enters. She is rather smarter than when we last saw her, a new and rather unsuitable hat. She carries several packages. She looks tired.*)
SALLY. Oh, hello, Chris. Hello, Fritz.
FRITZ. Hello, Sally. We were just admiring your picture.
SALLY. Oh, "The Kitten's Awakening." (*Moves in between them.*) I've had that ever since I was a child. It's a dead kitten waking up in Heaven—with angel kittens around.
CHRISTOPHER. Miaow, miaow. (*To the tune of "Noel, Noel."*)
SALLY. Chris makes awful fun of it. (*Hits Christopher on head with teddy bear, then moves over to table and puts parcels down.*) But I think it's rather sweet.
FRITZ. It is very sweet. (*Replaces picture and returns to above couch.*)
SALLY. Goodness, it's hot out, and it's late September already.
CHRISTOPHER. You are very dressy today.
SALLY. I am? Oh, this hat. Yes, it's new. Clive bought it for me. I don't like it much, but it cost so much money. (*Moves up to washstand and puts handbag down on chair* D. S. *of it.*) Let's have a Prairie Oyster. Will you, Chris?
CHRISTOPHER. No, I think they affect my back.
SALLY. Fritz?
FRITZ. I would like to try one.
SALLY. I'll make them. Chris doesn't really know how. (*Starts to do so, puts two glasses from washstand on table* L.)
FRITZ. (*Moving round to* R. *end of couch.*) And who is this Clive who gives you hats?
SALLY. He's an American. Chris and I met him a week ago at the Troika bar. We were both sitting alone, having a beer each because we were both so bloody miserable, and he was sitting next to us, and he ordered champagne for us all, (*Gets sauce from cupboard and brings it to table.*) and we didn't separate till four the

next morning. And ever since then we've hardly been apart, have we, Chris? (*Moves up to cupboard and kneels, opening it to look for eggs.*)

CHRISTOPHER. He's so rich, we daren't let him out of our sight.

FRITZ. And he is here just on vacation?

CHRISTOPHER. He lives on vacation. I've never seen anyone drink so much. (*Sally brings eggs down to table.*) He's unhappy, he says. But I've never really found out why. Have you, Sally?

SALLY. (*Pours sauce into glasses.*) Yes, dear. It's his wives. There have been four of them, and they none of them even liked him. And, before that, it was his peculiar grandfathers. They both brought him up six months each. One was a Baptist, and the other lived in Paris. So, no wonder it split him. (*Breaks eggs into glasses.*) He's rather an interesting character like out of Dostioffsky. He's sort of lost faith in everything, and I think Chris and I are putting it back, in bits. (*Throws egg shells into waste basket.*) That's why I feel all right about letting Clive give us things. There's a dozen pairs of silk stockings in there, Chris. And absolutely gallons of Chanel Five. Oh, and some shirts for you. Some silk shirts.

CHRISTOPHER. Good God.

SALLY. The colors are a bit outrageous, but they're the best silk. Where's something to stir this with? (*Fritz crosses round to* L. *of couch.*) Oh, this pen will do. (*Picks up a fountain pen and stirs the oysters.*) There. (*She hands one over to Fritz, and gulps down her own.*) Oh, that's marvellous. (*Licks pen.*) I feel better already. (*Puts pen down and goes up to washstand—takes hat off, then moves down to* L. *end of couch and sits. Fritz chokes.*) Well, how are things, Fritz? You know, Natalia came to see me several times, as though she were doing district visiting and I were a fallen woman or something. But she seems to have stopped.

FRITZ. She is away with her parents. She comes back next week, and then there is a surprise for her. Chris has told me your advice, that I should pounce on her, and I am going to take it. (*Takes another sip of his drink and chokes again.*)

SALLY. What's the matter? Don't you like your Prairie Oyster?

FRITZ. (*Puts glass down on table* L.) It is a little painful. You drink them all down at once?

SALLY. Yes, they're better that way. Especially when you are not feeling well. They sort of come back at you.

CHRISTOPHER. Aren't you feeling well, Sally?

SALLY. Not really.
FRITZ. You would like me to go?
SALLY. Fritz darling, would you mind terribly? I would like to lie down a bit. (*Christopher rises and moves round to head of couch.*)
FRITZ. But of course. With me there are no compliments. Sally, you lie down. (*Christopher and Fritz help Sally to lie down.*) Then you feel better. I go now. You take her to dinner, Chris, and cheer her up.
CHRISTOPHER. I'll try. Good-bye, Fritz. (*Fritz goes. Christopher gets Sally's slippers from beside the bed and brings them down.*) Sally, are you really feeling ill? (*Helps Sally on with slippers.*)
SALLY. Not so much ill, as just wanting to get rid of him. Fritz is sweet. I mean, he's an old friend, but I thought if I had to go on being bright any longer that I'd die. (*Christopher puts shoes beside bed.*) I've got something to tell you, Chris.
CHRISTOPHER. What is it?
SALLY. (*Sitting up.*) Chris, I went to the doctor this afternoon . . . and I'm going to have a baby.
CHRISTOPHER. (*Moving down to* L. *of her.*) Oh, my God!
SALLY. I've been afraid of it for a long time only I wouldn't think about it. I kept pretending it wasn't true. Then yesterday I was sick, and then I fainted this morning. And that's what made me go.
CHRISTOPHER. Is it Klaus's child?
SALLY. Yes.
CHRISTOPHER. Does he know?
SALLY. (*Sharply.*) No, he doesn't.
CHRISTOPHER. Well, you're going to tell him, aren't you?
SALLY. I don't know, Chris. I haven't heard from him for weeks and weeks. I wrote to him last week, the nicest letter I could, and he hasn't answered. Not a word. You didn't like him, did you?
CHRISTOPHER. I didn't really know him. I didn't think he was good enough for you. (*Sits* L. *of Sally.*)
SALLY. That's sweet of you. (*Rises.*)
CHRISTOPHER. But you're going to tell him this, now?
SALLY. (*Crossing to above table.*) No. Not if he doesn't write to me. I can't beg him. And that's what it would be like. I mean, I mayn't be up to much, but I do have some pride.
CHRISTOPHER. Well, what then . . . if he doesn't write?

SALLY. I don't know. That's what scares me. It's silly, Chris . . . it happens to other girls. Almost all other girls. But I am scared. Do you suppose they all are, too? (*A knock at the door.*)
SCHNEIDER. (*Off.*) It is I, Fräulein Sally. The post is here.
CHRISTOPHER. (*Sotto voce.*) She's been keeping an eye out for it.
SALLY. Come in.
SCHNEIDER. (*Entering and going to her.*) There is a letter for you. The one you want, from England.
SALLY. Oh, thank you.
SCHNEIDER. Ja, Fräulein. (*Schneider hands letter to Sally and waits. Sally starts to undo her packages. Schneider gives up and goes out. Sally waits for her to leave. Then she rips the letter open. Christopher stands by. She reads it. Her face changes.*)
CHRISTOPHER. What's the matter?
SALLY. It's what I thought. He's throwing me over.
CHRISTOPHER. (*Rises.*) Oh, no.
SALLY. Right over. With a whole lot of stuff about how badly he's behaved to me. (*Sally hands Christopher the first page. He reads it. She goes on with the second.*) Apparently there's someone else. A Lady Gore-Eckersley. He says she is wonderful. She's a virgin. A communist virgin. (*Lays the letter down.*) Well, those are two things no one could ever say of *me*.
CHRISTOPHER. (*Going to Sally and putting his arms around her.*) Oh, Sally, I'm sorry.
SALLY. (*Leaning against him.*) It's silly, isn't it?
CHRISTOPHER. It is a kind of bloody letter.
SALLY. I'm afraid he's rather a bloody person, really. Oh, Chris, I am a lousy picker. Always the duds who'll do me in.
CHRISTOPHER. I won't, Sally.
SALLY. I know. I suppose that's why I haven't been interested in you that way. (*Crosses to head of couch.*)
CHRISTOPHER. (*Moves in to* L. *of couch.*) Sally, you'll have to tell Klaus. He'll have to help you.
SALLY. What would be the good? He'd only run away. Leave no address. I knew this was going to happen. (*Turns to Christopher.*) I can't have the baby, Chris. It's awful, because I want to. But not unless I'm married, and can look after it.
CHRISTOPHER. (*After a second.*) I'll marry you, Sally.
SALLY. (*Turns away and sits on pouffe.*) Oh, Chris, what good

would that do? Klaus's child . . . and I'd be a rotten sort of mother. Just a betrayed whore.

CHRISTOPHER. (*Going to her. Sharply.*) Sally, for God's sake, stop calling yourself that. You know you're not.

SALLY. (*Bitterly.*) Yes, I am. Just that. One who's fallen in love with a swine, because he's her type, and then got caught. That's all. Just a whore and a fool. (*Starts to cry.*)

CHRISTOPHER. Sally, stop crying.

SALLY. I've got to find someone.

CHRISTOPHER. Won't this doctor . . . ?

SALLY. No. He was quite shocked when I told him I wasn't married.

CHRISTOPHER. Then we'll get someone. Maybe we should ask Fräulein Schneider.

SALLY. Do you think *she'd* know anyone?

CHRISTOPHER. She knows just about everything, I've always thought. I'll call her. (*Opens door. Sally moves away* U. L. *to washstand.*) Fräulein Schneider!

SCHNEIDER. (*Off.*) Ja.

CHRISTOPHER. Fräulein. Can you come in here? (*Comes back.*) It will be all right, Sally. I promise you. (*Schneider enters and comes in to head of couch.*)

SCHNEIDER. You called for me, Herr Issyvoo?

CHRISTOPHER. Yes. We need your advice. Do you want to tell her, Sally?

SALLY. (*Her back to them.*) No. You do it.

CHRISTOPHER. Well, you see, Fräulein Schneider, Sally is in a little bit of trouble . . .

SCHNEIDER. Ja?

CHRISTOPHER. She's going to have a baby.

SCHNEIDER. Um Gotteswillen.

CHRISTOPHER. So you see . . .

SCHNEIDER. But then this Herr Klaus, he will come back and marry her.

CHRISTOPHER. Well, you see, he isn't awfully anxious to. You see . . .

SALLY. (*Angrily, coming down to* L. *of couch.*) It isn't that at all, Chris. You never can tell anything right. It's I who doesn't want him, Fräulein. I don't ever want to see him again. (*Turns away from them.*)

SCHNEIDER. Ach, so . . .

CHRISTOPHER. So you see, we want to get—er—to get rid of the baby. The point is—do you know anyone?

SCHNEIDER. Yes, I do. There was a young lady living here once, and she went to the doctor.

SALLY. For the same thing?

SCHNEIDER. Exactly the same thing.

SALLY. And was it all right?

SCHNEIDER. It was quite all right. (*Crossing to Sally.*) I have his address and telephone number still. I kept it just in case it should ever happen again. (*Christopher sits on pouffe.*)

SALLY. (*Trying to be easy over it.*) I suppose it happens quite often, really?

SCHNEIDER. It can always happen. It is just bad luck. But he is rather expensive. It is a certificate he has to give that your health will not let you have the risk of childbirth. It costs money, that certificate.

SALLY. How much?

SCHNEIDER. For this other young lady, it was three hundred marks.

CHRISTOPHER. Three hundred!

SCHNEIDER. We could make it a little cheaper, I think, if we argued. Maybe two hundred and fifty.

CHRISTOPHER. That's still an awful lot.

SALLY. I know it is. But I've got to do it, Chris. I really have. (*Crosses to Schneider and takes her hands.*) You'd better ring up the doctor, Fräulein, and see if he can see us.

SCHNEIDER. You like that I come with you?

SALLY. Oh, would you? That would be marvellous. (*As Schneider crosses to door, Sally follows her.*) I say . . . Fräulein! Where—where does he do it?

SCHNEIDER. There is a nursing home. You stay there two or three days, and then you come back here and rest. In maybe ten days, no more, it is all forgotten. I go telephone. (*She goes out gaily.*)

SALLY. (*Crossing to couch and sitting on floor in front of it.*) It's like a treat to *her*.

CHRISTOPHER. It'll be all right, Sally, I know it will. The other girl was all right.

SALLY. There's something so *degrading* about it, as well as dan-

gerous. Oh, damn! Isn't it idiotic? All the men I've had, and there have been quite a lot, and this has to happen to me. It's awful, too, when you think about it, that there's something alive inside of you, that you can't have. That you mustn't have. It's like finding out that all the old rules are true, after all.
CHRISTOPHER. Sally, two hundred and fifty marks. And the home will probably cost a bit of money, too. I've started making a little more now, too. If I can help you . . .
SALLY. (*Turns to him.*) Oh, Chris, you are an angel. I'll pay you back. I swear I will. And you know, I think perhaps you had better come with us. We'll say you're the father. I think it looks better to have him along.
CHRISTOPHER. (*Comes to* R. *of Sally and sits on couch with arms round her.*) Yes, Sally, of course I'll come with you.
SALLY. Oh, Chris, I don't know what I'd do without you. (*She clings to Christopher and he holds her. Bell rings.*) Oh, damn, there's the bell. If it's anyone for me, I'm not home. I won't see anyone. (*Opens the door, and goes down the passage. Christopher rises and moves round to above couch.*) Fräulein Schneider, I'm not at home to anyone. I won't see . . . Oh, hello, Clive, come in.
CLIVE. (*Off.*) Hello, there. I just thought I'd come and look you up.
SALLY. (*Returning and crossing to* C.) It's Clive. (*Clive enters. He is in his late thirties, large, American, blond, and drunkish.*)
CLIVE. Well, hello, Chris, you son of a gun. (*Shakes hands.*)
CHRISTOPHER. Hello, Clive.
CLIVE. (*Crossing to Sally.*) I've never seen your place before. I thought I'd come and take a gander at it. I brought you these. (*Presents an enormous box of very expensive flowers.*)
SALLY. Oh, Clive, how wonderful of you. (*Clive looks round room.*) Look, Chris, from that terribly expensive shop on the Linden.
CHRISTOPHER. Goodness.
CLIVE. So this is where you live, eh? Just one room? Say, it's not very grand, is it? Can't you do better than this?
SALLY. I—er—I have in my time. This is just temporary. (*Takes ribbon off flower box.*)
CLIVE. Oh, sure. Sure.
CHRISTOPHER. (*Defensive.*) What's the matter with it?
CLIVE. Well, it's not exactly *de luxe*, do you think?

CHRISTOPHER. (*As before.*) I think it's very nice. (*Sally puts flower box on floor.*)
CLIVE. Oh, sure. Sure. I wasn't casting any slurs. I just thought maybe something a bit more modern. But it's okay. Say, I bet your rooms are better.
SALLY. Oh, yes, they're much better. They're wonderful.
CLIVE. Where are they?
CHRISTOPHER. Just across the hall.
CLIVE. (*Going to door.*) Mind if I take a look? (*Sally starts to gesture wildly at Christopher not to show his room.*)
CHRISTOPHER. (*Stopping him.*) Well—er—they're rather untidy just now.
CLIVE. That's all right with me. (*Sally repeats her gesture.*)
CHRISTOPHER. There are some things lying around that—well, that I wouldn't want anyone to see.
CLIVE. Say, what are those?
CHRISTOPHER. Just some personal things.
CLIVE. (*Starting to go again.*) Boy, that's what I'd like to look at.
CHRISTOPHER. I'm awfully sorry, but I don't think . . .
CLIVE. You mean, you've got someone in there?
CHRISTOPHER. Well, er . . .
CLIVE. (*Pushing Christopher towards door.*) Why don't you come right out and say it, feller? Don't beat about the bush. Go on back to her. I'll understand.
CHRISTOPHER. (*Again on a gesture from Sally.*) Well, she's—er—asleep just now.
CLIVE. And, boy, I bet she needs it. Well, say, now what have you got in the way of liquor? (*Sally makes room for Clive on couch. He sits* R. *of her.*)
SALLY. We've got some gin.
CHRISTOPHER. Not much. (*Goes to door and shuts it.*)
SALLY. I'm afraid we're out of whisky.
CLIVE. Say, you need some stores. I'll send you in a cellar. (*Rises and moves away* U. S.) Now, look, what are we going to do? I've been all by myself all day, and it's driving me nuts. There's a place I've heard of out on the Wannsee. The Regina Palast Garten. (*Comes down to above Sally and ruffles her hair.*) I thought we might drive out there for dinner.
SALLY. The three of us.

CLIVE. (*To Christopher.*) If you're free. (*Sally nods at Christopher.*)
CHRISTOPHER. Oh, yes, I'll be free.
CLIVE. (*Moves in to* L. *of Christopher.*) Is that a good place?
CHRISTOPHER. I've always heard it was.
CLIVE. But you've never been there?
CHRISTOPHER. It's much too expensive for us.
CLIVE. Well, fine. Only is it *really* a good place? Can we have a good time there? The real McCoy?
SALLY. It's about the best place there is.
CLIVE. Oh, well, swell, then. That's great. That's the *real* thing. Well, shall we go?
SALLY. I can't go yet.
CLIVE. Why, what have you got on? (*Schneider enters and crosses* D. S. *to* R. *of pouffe.*)
SCHNEIDER. Fräulein Sally, can I speak to you a moment, please?
CLIVE. (*Crossing to Schneider.*) That's all right. You speak up. No secrets here. No secrets in front of Uncle Clive.
SALLY. (*Rises.*) Have you talked to the—to the man, Fräulein?
SCHNEIDER. He says he can see you right away.
SALLY. Oh—oh, thanks.
SCHNEIDER. It takes twenty minutes from here. I think perhaps you should go now.
SALLY. Oh, yes, I will. You get your hat and coat, Fräulein, and I'll be ready.
SCHNEIDER. Ja, Fräulein. (*Exit.*)
CLIVE. (*Crossing to Sally.*) What man is this?
SALLY. It's just a man about a job. A sort of audition.
CLIVE. I'll drive you there.
SALLY. I don't think you'd better. I mean, it's not a very big job, and it would look a little funny if I were to arrive in a Dusenberg car.
CLIVE. It would make them pay you more. (*Christopher moves down to couch.*)
SALLY. Look, Clive, it's awfully sweet of you, but I think we'd better go by bus.
CLIVE. You take your landlady on auditions with you?
SALLY. Sometimes. She gives me confidence.
CLIVE. (*Crossing to* R. *of Christopher.*) Well, then, Chris and I

will go to the Adlon, and sit in the bar and wait for you. He can bring his girl along, if he wants to.
CHRISTOPHER. Oh, no, that's all right. But—I've got to go out, too, and then I've got to come back here for just a minute. Why don't we all meet later at the Adlon? (*Slaps Clive on the arms.*)
CLIVE. I'll send my car back here for you. Six o'clock? (*He slaps Christopher on the arms.*)
CHRISTOPHER. Fine. (*He slaps Clive on the arms.*)
SALLY. That would be wonderful. And thank you so much for these.
CLIVE. (*Crosses to Sally and takes her hand.*) Well, good luck. I hope you get the job.
SALLY. I do, too. (*Turns away.*) At least, I—I think I do.
CLIVE. We'll celebrate tonight, if you do. And if you don't, well, then we'll tie a bun on anyway, just to forget it all. So either way, you can't lose. So long, Chris, you sexy old bastard. (*Exit.*)
SALLY. (*Crosses to couch and sits.*) Oh, Chris, I thought we were never going to get rid of him.
CHRISTOPHER. Yes, so did I. You know, he is an extraordinary man.
SALLY. But he's awfully sweet, really. Perhaps, when this is over, I can devote myself to him. I've always thought I'd like to have a really rich man for a lover. Or perhaps I could marry him, and then I might reform him. I could, you know, I really could.
CHRISTOPHER. Sally, do you really think you could reform anyone?
SALLY. Oh, Chris, don't. Don't pull me down again. I feel awful.
CHRISTOPHER. (*Crosses to behind couch and sits on arm.*) I'm sorry, Sally. And don't worry about reforming people. You're sweet. You really are.
SALLY. Thank you, Chris. Even if you don't mean it.
CHRISTOPHER. But I do. (*Rises and goes up to bed for her shoes.*) And now we'd better get going.
SALLY. Yes, I suppose so. (*Christopher helps Sally on with her shoes.*) I suppose we should put these flowers in water. (*She picks up box.*) They cost such a lot. I'll just put them in the bath for now. Then I'll see if Fräulein Schneider is ready, and come back for my hat. (*Goes to the door, and turns to Christopher.*) Thank you for offering to marry me. (*Exit.*)
CHRISTOPHER. (*Sally's slippers in his hand.*) And this is the

kind of thing we used to make dirty jokes about at school. The facts of life. And here we go to prove they're not true, or that you can dodge them. (*Drops the slippers.*) And then we'll get pounds and pounds spent on us for dinner. And drink too much. And try to believe that none of it matters anyway. (*Gets a cigarette from his pocket.*) And soon, as Fräulein Schneider said, we'll forget the whole thing. And we won't believe or remember a thing about it. Either of us. (*Starts to put the cigarette in his mouth. Then he stops and looks at the door.*) Or will we?

CURTAIN

ACT II

SCENE 1

Ten days later.

Christopher is alone, sitting on the pouffe, D. L. *now, pasting photographs in an album. The couch has been moved to the window and the table to the center of the room. The large chair has been placed at the* R. *of the table. There is another chair to the* L. *of the table.*

CHRISTOPHER. (*To himself.*) This awful, obscene laziness! I ought to be flogged. Where has the time gone to? Jittering helplessly over the bad news in the papers, staring half-drunk at my reflection in the mirrors of bars, skimming crime-novels, hunting for sex. Summer's almost over. Instead of ripening like an apple, I'm wearing out like an old boot. This place stinks of my failure. (*Sally comes back into the room. She wears a robe and looks pale and ill.*) Are you all right?

SALLY. Yes, I'm all right. Just. Goodness, if it takes all that effort, just to go across the hall. (*Pausing behind Christopher, she ruffles his hair.*) How's all your creeping paralysis, Chris?

CHRISTOPHER. Oh, that's gone. (*Feeling his left side.*) But you know, I think I've got appendicitis.

SALLY. (*Crossing to couch and settling down to a half-finished game of patience.*) If you have, you just die of it. Don't let them operate on you. You know, Chris, what I would really like would be some champagne. Some really cold champagne.

CHRISTOPHER. I'm afraid we haven't got any of that.

SALLY. Clive ought to have sent us whole baskets of it. I do think it was odd his disappearing like he did. Where do you think he went, Chris?

CHRISTOPHER. I wonder if he didn't go off on an opium jag.

SALLY. That's quite possible. I never thought of that. Oh dear, I've known a lot of opium fiends, and you never could really rely

on them. And then what happens to my career?
CHRISTOPHER. Do you really think he's going to do anything about that?
SALLY. He says he's going to put up all the money for a show for me. All I've got to do now is find the show. And then find *him* again. But until he shows up we don't get any champagne, and I do want some. I want some terribly, now I've thought about it.
CHRISTOPHER. I'd buy you some, if I could, Sally. But you know we really are desperately broke.
SALLY. You know, Chris, in some ways now I wish I had had that kid. The last day or two, I've been sort of feeling what it would be like to be a mother. Do you know, last night I sat here for a long time by myself, and held this teddy bear in my arms, and imagined it was my baby? I felt a most marvellous sort of shut-off feeling from all the rest of the world. I imagined how it would grow up, and how after I'd put it to bed at nights, I'd go out and make love to filthy old men to get money to pay for its clothes and food.
CHRISTOPHER. You mean, a baby would be your purpose in life?
SALLY. Yes, I wouldn't think of myself at all. Just it. It must be rather wonderful never to think of yourself, just of someone else. I suppose that's what people mean by religion. Do you think I could be a nun, Chris? I really rather think I could. All pale and pious, singing sort of faint and lovely hymns all day long.
CHRISTOPHER. I think you'd get tired of it. You'd better just marry and have a child.
SALLY. I feel as if I'd lost faith in men. Even you, Christopher, if you were to go out into the street now, and be run over by a taxi . . . I should be sorry in a way, of course, but I shouldn't really care a damn.
CHRISTOPHER. (*Laughing.*) Thank you, Sally.
SALLY. (*Moving to him and kneeling on floor* L. *of him.*) I didn't mean that, of course, darling—at least, not personally. You mustn't mind what I say when I'm like this. I can see now why people say operations like that are wrong. They are. You know the whole business of having children is all wrong. It's a most wonderful thing, and it ought to be the result of something very rare and special and sort of privileged, instead of just *that!* What are you grinning about?

CHRISTOPHER. Well, that's what it's supposed to be. The result of something rare and special. That's what *that's* supposed to be. (*Closes album.*)
SALLY. Oh, goodness, is it? Yes, I suppose it *is* supposed to be. Oh, is *that* why people say it's wrong to do it when you're not married, or terribly deeply in love?
CHRISTOPHER. Yes, of course it is. (*Rises and puts album and paste on chair by washstand.*)
SALLY. Well, why didn't anyone ever *tell* me?
CHRISTOPHER. (*Comes down to* R. *of pouffe and sits on floor.*) I expect they did, and you didn't believe them.
SALLY. Did *you* believe them when they told you?
CHRISTOPHER. No, Sally. I don't think we'll ever quite trust things, in the long run.
SALLY. I trust you, Chris. I'm terribly fond of you.
CHRISTOPHER. I'm fond of you too, Sally.
SALLY. And you're not in love with me, are you?
CHRISTOPHER. No, I'm not in love with you.
SALLY. I'm awfully glad. I wanted you to like me from the first minute we met. But I'm glad you're not in love with me. Somehow or other, I couldn't possibly be in love with you . . . So, if you had been, everything would have spoiled. Hold my hand, Chris, and let's swear eternal friendship.
CHRISTOPHER. (*Taking her hand across the pouffe.*) I swear eternal friendship.
SALLY. So do I. (*The bell rings. They both rise, and Christopher pushes pouffe up about two feet.*) Oh, dear, I wonder who that is. I hope it's no one for us. I'd much rather be alone with you, Chris.
CHRISTOPHER. So would I, Sally.
SALLY. (*Sits on couch.*) Oh, Chris, don't go and get run over by a taxi. (*Schneider enters.*)
SCHNEIDER. It is Fräulein Landauer to see you, Fräulein. (*Natalia enters and crosses to Sally, ignoring Christopher.*)
CHRISTOPHER. Hello, Natalia.
NATALIA. Fräulein Bowles, I am but just back from the country and I have only just heard that you have not been well. So I have hurried in to see you.
SALLY. That's very nice of you.
NATALIA. (*Turning.*) Oh, hello, Christopher.

CHRISTOPHER. Hello, Natalia.
NATALIA. (*To Sally.*) I bring you these few flowers.
SALLY. Oh, thank you so much. (*Hands flowers to Christopher.*) Chris . . . Won't you sit down? (*Christopher takes the flowers. Natalia sits on pouffe.*)
NATALIA. Thank you. What is, please, that has been the matter with you?
CHRISTOPHER. (*Quickly.*) Oh, just a little ulcer, that's all. They had to cut it out.
NATALIA. Where was the ulcer?
SALLY. Inside.
NATALIA. But, of course, it was inside. Where, please, inside?
SALLY. I don't really know. In here, somewhere.
NATALIA. And who, please, was it who cut it out for you?
SALLY. The doctor.
NATALIA. But yes, it was the doctor. I did not think it was the sewing-lady. What doctor is it you go to?
SALLY. Oh, just a doctor—a very good doctor. Would you like some coffee or anything?
NATALIA. Yes, I think that I would like some coffee.
SALLY. Will you get it, Chris? (*Christopher crosses to door.*)
NATALIA. (*Rising and crossing to table. Puts bag and gloves down.*) And, Christopher, if you could stay away for just a little while, it would be nice, too. I have something that I wish to say to Fräulein Bowles. (*Sally rises and crosses to table.*)
CHRISTOPHER. Yes, of course. (*Goes out. Sally offers Natalia a cigarette.*)
NATALIA. No, thank you. (*Goes to couch and sits.*) Tell me, Fräulein, please, have you seen Fritz Wendel lately?
SALLY. (*Takes cigarette and lights it.*) Not for the last day or so.
NATALIA. I come back from the country two days before yesterday. He comes to call on me that evening. Fräulein, I think I have done you perhaps an injustice.
SALLY. Oh?
NATALIA. I have always think of you as a young lady who has no control of herself, and I have been disdainful of you therefrom. I am sorry. I do not think I quite understood.
SALLY. How do you mean?
NATALIA. I have think always that I have control of myself.

Please, you will not laugh at me if I tell you something that is very personal to me?
SALLY. No, of course I won't. (*Crosses to pouffe and sits.*)
NATALIA. Fräulein Bowles, Fritz Wendel has made love to me, and I have not taken him seriously, because it's all too formal, too discreet. Then, two nights before last, it is all changed. He throws aside his formality, and it is quite different. I have never known a man like that. And it has disturbed me. I cannot sleep for it. And that is not like me.
SALLY. But what am I supposed to tell you?
NATALIA. (*Rises and crosses to* L. *of Sally.*) I wish to know, please, if I should marry him. My parents tell me no. They care for me. They think only of me, and they do not care for him. And he is not Jewish, and they wish that I should marry a Jewish man. I have always wished so, myself. Now I do not care. Only I think perhaps there is something of Herr Wendel's life that I do not know, that perhaps you do. And that therefore I should not marry him. You will tell me, please?
SALLY. Yes, I . . . I think perhaps there is.
NATALIA. What, please?
SALLY. I . . . I don't think I can tell you, exactly. But I don't really think he's your kind. I don't really think you ought to marry him—not if you ask me like that, point-blank.
NATALIA. I do not think so, too. (*Returns to couch and sits.*) But I think if I do not, that perhaps I will kill myself.
SALLY. Oh, no, you won't.
NATALIA. I do not think you know me. I do not think I know myself. (*Begins to cry.*)
SALLY. Oh, there's nothing to cry about. (*Rises, goes to table and puts cigarette out. Natalia goes on crying.*) Oh, don't. Please don't. You'll have me crying, too. I'm most frightfully weak still, and I cry over almost anything.
NATALIA. (*Still crying.*) I am sorry. I did not know that love was like this. It is not what the poets have said. It is awful, and it is degrading.
SALLY. Yes, I know. It is. It's absolutely awful when it really hits you. But you mustn't give in to it, really you mustn't. I know that sounds silly coming from me. (*Goes to Natalia and kneels on floor by her.*) But what do you think has been the matter with

me? I was going to have a baby, and the chap let me down, and I had to get rid of it.

NATALIA. (*Turning, amazed.*) Oh, I am sorry. I did not know.

SALLY. And marriage isn't going to make it any better if it's not the right man.

NATALIA. You think, then, that I must be strong?

SALLY. Yes, I do.

NATALIA. I think so. too. (*Rises, crossing to between table and pouffe.*) But, um Gotteswillen! What is there to *do* with one's life, all of a sudden?

SALLY. You could become a nun. Do they have Jewish nuns? (*Christopher taps on the door.*)

CHRISTOPHER. (*Off.*) The coffee is ready.

NATALIA. You may come in now. (*Natalia turns her back, and straightens her face in the mirror above washstand. Christopher comes in with coffee. Sally sits on couch.*)

CHRISTOPHER. I only brought one cup. Sally doesn't take it, and I think I'm getting allergic to it, too.

NATALIA. You are very kind, but I do not think now that I have time. (*She turns and crosses to door, picking up bag, etc., from table.*) So, Christopher, we will start our lessons again now? I think now that I will perhaps take more. I will take two every day. You can manage that?

CHRISTOPHER. Yes, I can manage it. But that is an awful lot for you. It's an awful lot to do.

NATALIA. I need an awful lot to do. Good-bye, Fräulein. I thank you, and I come again. (*Goes out, rather hurriedly.*)

CHRISTOPHER. What was all that about?

SALLY. (*Very nobly and remotely.*) That was something personal. That poor girl is terribly unhappy.

CHRISTOPHER. What about?

SALLY. (*As before.*) This is something between women. (*Christopher giggles and sits on chair* L. *of table.*) It is. I've given her some advice. Some very good advice.

CHRISTOPHER. You gave Fritz some advice, too.

SALLY. Oh, I did, didn't I? Oh, that was awful. Because it paid off. I'm never going to be funny and flippant again. (*Rises and crosses to Christopher.*) I'm going to be dead serious, and take everyone's problems to heart. I am, Chris. I wish you wouldn't sit

there and snigger like that. You don't know how silly it makes you look. (*Bell rings.*)
CHRISTOPHER. I'm a bit on your nerves, aren't I, Sally?
SALLY. (*Goes to window.*) Yes, you are. Oh, it's not only you. It's everyone. I'm on my own nerves.
SCHNEIDER. (*Opening door.*) Fräulein Sally, hier ist der Herr Americaner. Bitte, mein Herr. Bitte sehr. (*Clive comes in. He carries a basket of champagne, which he gives to Christopher.*)
CLIVE. Well, hello, hello, hello, there.
SALLY. Well, hello, Clive.
CHRISTOPHER. Hello. (*Rises and moves to below table. Handshakes are performed.*)
SALLY. We thought you'd forgotten all about us. (*Christopher puts champagne on table.*)
CLIVE. Oh, for God's sake, no. Say, I've only just heard you'd been sick. Why didn't you let me know?
SALLY. You weren't around.
CLIVE. (*Sits by Sally.*) What was the matter with you, anyway?
SALLY. I had an operation.
CLIVE. Oh, gee, that's tough. How are you feeling now?
SALLY. Better. Much better. Now that I've seen you.
CLIVE. Well, that's fine. Feel like coming out to dinner tonight?
SALLY. I can't do that. It's all I can do to get to the bathroom.
CLIVE. Ah, come on. Do you good.
CHRISTOPHER. She can't, Clive. She really can't walk yet.
CLIVE. (*Rising.*) Oh, hell, anyone can walk if they want to.
CHRISTOPHER. No, she mustn't. Really.
CLIVE. Well, let's have dinner up here, then. All of us. I brought you some champagne.
SALLY. Oh, Clive, how wonderful of you. I was just saying to Chris that what I'd like best in the world would be some champagne.
CLIVE. (*Crossing to Christopher above table* C.) Well, let's have it. It's still good and cold. I only just got it. Open it, will you, Chris, there's a good feller?
CHRISTOPHER. I'll just get another glass from my room. (*Goes out taking coffee tray.*)
CLIVE. Well, let's take a look at you. (*Crosses to Sally and kneels on couch.*) Gee, you're a pale little lady. We'll have to pack you off some place to perk you up a bit. Where would you like to go?

SALLY. Clive, I think maybe I ought to stay here for my career.
CLIVE. (*Vaguely.*) Your career?
SALLY. Yes, the theatre.
CLIVE. Oh, sure, sure. (*Sits on pouffe.*)
SALLY. I mean, if I am going to do a play, we ought to start thinking and planning a bit quite soon.
CLIVE. Oh, plenty of time for that. Get you well first. (*Christopher returns with three tooth glasses and puts them on table.*)
SALLY. I'll be all right in a few days.
CLIVE. Get you really well.
SALLY. No, but, Clive, I do think . . .
CLIVE. You leave that all to me. Leave that all to Uncle Clive. (*To Christopher.*) Say, are those the best glasses you can manage?
CHRISTOPHER. I think Fräulein Schneider may have some others.
SALLY. (*Rises.*) Don't bother, darling. All I want is the champagne. Open it, won't you?
CHRISTOPHER. All right. (*Starts to do so. Takes one bottle out and puts basket on floor.*)
SALLY. Where have you been, Clive? (*Puts her arms round Clive.*)
CLIVE. Been?
SALLY. You've been away somewhere, haven't you?
CLIVE. Ah, just for a day or two.
SALLY. It's been ten days.
CLIVE. Has it? Yeah, it may have been. (*Rises and moves away* L. *Sally sits on pouffe.*) I can never keep track of time when I'm on a bat. You know, this is a funny city. (*Looking out of window.*) Driving here, just now, we ran right into a bit of shooting.
CHRISTOPHER. Shooting?
CLIVE. Seemed just like Chicago. (*Comes down to above chair* L.)
CHRISTOPHER. Where was this?
CLIVE. I don't know. Right in front of one of the big department stores. (*Sits.*) Birnbaum's, I think, where we bought you those fancy undies.
CHRISTOPHER. That's a Jewish store. That would be Nazi rioting, I imagine.
CLIVE. Say, who are these Nazis, anyway? I keep reading the word in the papers when I look at them, and I never know who they are referring to. Are the Nazis the same as the Jews?

CHRISTOPHER. No—they're—well, they're more or less the opposite. (*The champagne bottle is opened.*)
SALLY. Oh, that looks wonderful.
CLIVE. And there's a funeral going on today, too.
SALLY. Darling, isn't there always?
CLIVE. No, but this is the real thing. This is a real elegant funeral. It's been going on for over an hour. With banners and streamers, and God knows what all. I wonder who the guy was? He must have been a real swell.
CHRISTOPHER. (*Passing glasses.*) He was an old liberal leader. They put him in prison once for trying to stop the war. So now everybody loves him.
SALLY. Oh, this is marvellous. Just what the doctor ordered. Let's drink to Clive. (*Rises.*) Our best friend.
CHRISTOPHER. (*Rises.*) To Clive. (*They all drink.*)
CLIVE. (*Rises and crosses to table.*) Well, thank you both. I'll drink to the pair of you. Two real good playmates. (*Does so and pours himself another.*)
SALLY. You know I think there's something almost sacred about champagne. I think it's absolutely right that it's as expensive as it is. It makes one appreciate it more, like something really special. Like . . .
CHRISTOPHER. Like—*that!*
SALLY. Yes, exactly like *that.*
CLIVE. What's *that?* (*Christopher sits on couch.*)
SALLY. (*Vaguely noble.*) Oh—love and that sort of thing.
CLIVE. (*Leaning on table.*) You know, this is a pretty dreary sort of town. I've been here three weeks, and I'm getting kind of fed up with it.
SALLY. (*Alarmed.*) You're not going away?
CLIVE. I was kinda thinking of it.
SALLY. (*Rises and crosses to* L. *of Clive.*) Oh, no, Clive. You mustn't.
CLIVE. (*Suddenly.*) What do you say we *all* go? All three of us.
CHRISTOPHER. But where?
CLIVE. Where would you like to go?
CHRISTOPHER. (*As in a game.*) Anywhere in the world?
CLIVE. Anywhere in the world.
CHRISTOPHER. I think I'd like to go to India.
SALLY. Oh, no, it's all so terribly unsanitary. I want to go some-

where terrifically mysterious and sinister, and full of history. I'd like to go to Egypt.
CLIVE. (*Refills glasses.*) We can do both. Say, what do you say—we take off from here as soon as Sally's well enough? Take the Orient Express.
SALLY. That's such a lovely name.
CLIVE. Take it as far as Athens. Then we can fly to Egypt. Then back to Marseilles. From there we can get a boat to South America. Then Tahiti. Singapore. Japan.
CHRISTOPHER. You know, you manage to say those names as though they were stations on the subway!
SALLY. Well, he's been to them all heaps of times, haven't you, Clive darling?
CLIVE. Sure. Sure, I have. But I'd kind of get a kick out of showing them to you two kids. And then we can end up in California.
CHRISTOPHER. (*Rises.*) You don't mean it, do you, Clive? Just take off and go, just like that?
SALLY. (*Moves over to pouffe, then back to chair* L. *of table and kneels on it.*) But of course, Chris. Why ever not? This is sheer absolute heaven.
CHRISTOPHER. And what happens to your stage career?
SALLY. Oh, that can wait. Or we can pick it up again in California. I'm sure Clive knows all the picture magnates, don't you, Clive?
CLIVE. I know quite a few of them.
SALLY. I mean, you could get me on the films like that, if you wanted to?
CLIVE. Oh, I guess so. Well, what about it? When shall we take off? You won't need more than a week, will you? You can rest on the train.
SALLY. I can rest anywhere.
CLIVE. How's about a week from today?
SALLY. I think it would be marvellous.
CLIVE. (*To Christopher.*) All right with you?
CHRISTOPHER. (*Sitting down on pouffe, helplessly.*) Yes, I—I suppose so.
CLIVE. (*Rises and goes to* R. *of table.*) Okay, that's that, then. And, look, if we're going to have dinner up here, I'd better go get us a few things. What would you like? Some caviare. to start with?
SALLY. Oh, I'd adore that.

CLIVE. Then some soup. Some green turtle, maybe. And a partridge. With salad, of course. And I guess some of that chestnut ice cream with whipped cream all over it. And some fruit—some peaches.
SALLY. Get something for Fräulein Schneider.
CHRISTOPHER. Get her a pineapple. It's her idea of real luxury.
CLIVE. (*Starts moving to door.*) I think maybe we'd better get some new china, too, and some decent glasses.
CHRISTOPHER. Well, if we're going away next week . . .
CLIVE. Oh, heck, you can present them to your landlady to make up for your rent. I'll go get them.
SALLY. Why don't you send your chauffeur?
CLIVE. Heck no, this is kinda fun. Something to do. I'll get some real good brandy, too—half a dozen bottles—and we'll make a real picnic of it. So long, kids. I'll be right back. (*Exit. A long silence.*)
SALLY. Isn't life extraordinary? (*Goes to head of couch and looks out of window.*) Just when you think you've really touched bottom, something always turns up.
CHRISTOPHER. Do you think he means it?
SALLY. Yes, of course he does. (*Comes back to couch and kneels on it.*) You know, Chris, I really do adore him. I mean that. I really do.
CHRISTOPHER. I know. I've watched you doing it.
SALLY. You're looking all stunned. What's the matter?
CHRISTOPHER. I feel stunned. Doesn't it stun you when someone comes along and just whirls you right out of the whole flux of your life?
SALLY. (*Lies down.*) No, dear, not a bit. Besides, my life hasn't got a flux. And I don't think yours has, either.
CHRISTOPHER. No, you're right, it hasn't.
SALLY. Well, then?
CHRISTOPHER. But what will become of us?
SALLY. We shall have a wonderful time.
CHRISTOPHER. And then?
SALLY. I don't know. Oh, stop bothering with it, Chris. You always spoil things so.
CHRISTOPHER. We shall never come back.
SALLY. I don't want to come back.
CHRISTOPHER. I suppose you'll marry him.

SALLY. Of course I will.
CHRISTOPHER. And I? What will I be?
SALLY. You'll be a sort of private secretary, or something.
CHRISTOPHER. Without any duties. (*Sally lights cigarette. Christopher goes to table and puts glass down.*) You know, Sally, I can suddenly see myself ten years from now, in flannels and black-and-white shoes, pouring out drinks in the lounge of a California hotel. (*Crosses to window.*) I'll be a bit glassy in the eyes, and a lot heavier round the jowls.
SALLY. You'll have to take a lot of exercise, that's all.
CHRISTOPHER. (*At window.*) You were both quite right. We've got nothing to do with these Germans down there, or the shooting, or the funeral, with the dead man in his coffin, or the words on the banners. (*Goes to chair* R. *of table and sits.*) You know, in a few days, we shall have forfeited all kinship with about ninety-nine per cent of the world's population. The men and women who earn their livings, and insure their lives, and are anxious about the future of their children.
SALLY. It's the only way to live. Isn't there something in the Bible about "Take no thought for the morrow"? That's exactly what it means.
CHRISTOPHER. I think in the Middle Ages, people must have felt like this when they believed they had sold themselves to the devil.
SALLY. Well, you needn't come, if you don't want to.
CHRISTOPHER. Oh, no, I shall come. It's a funny feeling. Sort of exhilarating. Not really unpleasant. And yet, I'm frightened, too. If I do this, I'm lost. And yet I'm going to do it.
SALLY. (*Rises, crosses to chair* L. *of table and kneels.*) Darling, is there any more of that champagne?
CHRISTOPHER. Yes.
SALLY. Well, let's have it! (*Christopher pours it out.*) Chris, this is the end of one life, and the beginning of another. Two weeks from now, we'll probably be floating down the Nile, with the desert all round us in the moonlight, and all those marvellous sensual Arabs watching us from the tops of the pyramids. And then there'll be India. And a Maharajah will offer me my weight in diamonds if I'll spend one night in his harem.
CHRISTOPHER. You'd better put on some weight. Will you do it?

SALLY. (*Sits.*) Well, not unless he's one of the kind who looks like a sort of mixture of Valentino and Buddha. If you know what I mean.
CHRISTOPHER. Well, not exactly. What will I be doing all this time?
SALLY. Oh, you'll be looking simply marvellous and sexy in jodhpurs and an explorer's hat. And then there'll be feasts on volcanoes in the South Seas, and cocktails with Garbo. (*Pours more drinks and rises.*) Chris, what is it they say in German when you're going on a journey, and they want to wish you luck?
CHRISTOPHER. (*Rises.*) Hals and Beinbruch.
SALLY. What does that mean?
CHRISTOPHER. Neck and leg-break. It's supposed to stop you having them.
SALLY. That's wonderful. (*Raising her glass.*) Neck and leg-break, Chris.
CHRISTOPHER. Neck and leg-break. (*They drink.*)

CURTAIN

ACT II

SCENE 2

Five days later.
When the curtain rises, Christopher is seated at the table writing a letter. There are one or two dress boxes lying around, and an open suitcase in front of the bed.

CHRISTOPHER. (*Reading a P.S. to his letter.*) Next address: Poste Restante; The World. (*Schneider enters, carrying a large package, and crosses to* R. *of table.*)
SCHNFIDER. Herr Issyvoo, there is a box for you from Landauer's shop. I bring it in here, because the man has not come yet to repair the ceiling in your room. I think perhaps it is the news that has stopped him.
CHRISTOPHER.. (*Crosses to couch and sits*). What news?
SCHNEIDER. (*Crosses to pouffe.*) They have closed the National Bank. There will be thousands ruined, I shouldn't wonder. Such times we live in! It was bad during the war. Then they promise

us it will be better. And now it is almost worse again. (*To* R. *of table.*) It is the Jews. I know it is the Jews.

CHRISTOPHER. Fräulein Schneider, how can it be? You don't know what you are saying.

SCHNEIDER. They are too clever. And you buy things at Landauer's shop. That is a Jewish shop. What did you buy?

CHRISTOPHER. (*Opening the parcel.*) I bought a suit. It's—it's a tropical suit. (*Rises and crosses to* L. *of pouffe. With determination.*) Fräulein Schneider, there is something that I have got to tell you. I should have told you before; Fräulein Sally and I are going away. We're going—well, right round the world. We're leaving on Thursday.

SCHNEIDER. *This* Thursday? The day after tomorrow?

CHRISTOPHER. Yes, I'm afraid so. We'll pay you till the end of the month, of course.

SCHNEIDER. (*Sits in chair* L. *of table.*) But, Herr Issyvoo, this is dreadful. Both of you going away, and my other rooms empty, too. And now, with the banks closing, what shall I do?

CHRISTOPHER. (*Crosses to above table.*) I'm terribly sorry, but there are other tenants. There must be.

SCHNEIDER. How shall I live? And you tell me now, at the last minute!

CHRISTOPHER. I know. I'm sorry, but—you can have all that new china and glass we have.

SCHNEIDER. (*In an outburst.*) Never, never did I think it would come to this. To live on other people, to become fond of them, as I have of you. To help Fräulein Sally, take her to the doctor, and then to have you walk out like this, as though I were nothing but a landlady to whom you can fling the rent.

CHRISTOPHER. (*Helplessly.*) Fräulein Schneider, it's not that . . .

SCHNEIDER. And now I am an old woman, and nobody will care what becomes of me. I can go drown myself in the Spree. (*She is crying now. Christopher touches her.*)

CHRISTOPHER. Oh, please, Fräulein Schneider . . .

SCHNEIDER. (*Springing up and crossing to above pouffe.*) No, do not touch me. It is the Judas touch. (*Sally comes in. She wears a new light suit, carries another dress box and is very gay. She crosses to* R. *of chair* R. *of table.*)

SALLY. What on earth's going on?

CHRISTOPHER. I've just broken it to Fräulein Schneider that we're leaving. I am afraid that she is rather upset.
SCHNEIDER. Upset? Yes, I am upset. You go off on a trip of the whole world. You can afford to do that. But me, I have had to wait for my money, because you were too hard up sometimes to pay me. And now you throw me the china and glass as a tip. The china and the glass . . . I will throw them from the windows after your taxi as you go away. (*At door.*) That is what I think from your china and your glass. And from you, too. (*Exit.*)
SALLY. You're quite right, Chris. (*Puts parcels down.*) She *is* upset. What did you have to tell her for? (*Closes door. Sally crosses to bed and puts bag down. Christopher crosses to couch and sits.*)
CHRISTOPHER. Well, I thought we had to. It's only two days now. You know, that was sort of awful what she said about our being able to afford this trip.
SALLY. (*Comes down to table.*) I don't see why.
CHRISTOPHER. It doesn't seem wrong to you—to let Clive pay it all?
SALLY. Well, we couldn't do it, if he didn't. And he *wants to.* I mean, we didn't *ask* for it. (*The bell rings.*).
CHRISTOPHER. I didn't feel that I could quite explain that to Fräulein Schneider.
SALLY. I've got an absolutely exquisite *négligée.* I must show it to you. (*Opens the box, and takes out a fluffy pink négligée, with which she crosses to above pouffe and then displays.*) Look, isn't it simply marvellous?
CHRISTOPHER. But, Sally, what are you going to need that for?
SALLY. Darling, to lie around in.
CHRISTOPHER. Where?
SALLY. Anywhere. I expect we'll do lots of lying around. (*Schneider, quite grim now, announces.*)
SCHNEIDER. Herr Wendel. (*Fritz enters and crosses to below table. Schneider retires.*)
FRITZ. Well, then, hello, you.
SALLY. Hello. Look, Fritz, don't you think this is wonderful? (*Displays the négligé, jumping on the ottoman to do so.*)
FRITZ. But, yes. That is extremely seductive. It is for a part in the movies?
SALLY. No, it's to wear. We're going away, Fritz. Clive is taking

us. All around the world. We're leaving on Thursday. (*Goes up to the bed and puts négligé down on it.*)
FRITZ. You say again, please. (*Sally comes back for dress box and puts it down on bed.*)
CHRISTOPHER. We're going round the world.
FRITZ. (*Moves in to between couch and pouffe.*) The two of you. (*Sally and Chritsopher nod.*) With Clive?
CHRISTOPHER. I know, Fritz. It doesn't sound likely. But he did ask us.
SALLY. (*Crosses to above table for cigarette.*) Chris, do we have any of that champagne left?
CHRISTOPHER. Oh, yes, there are still about four bottles. You know he brought a dozen.
SALLY. Let's open one.
CHRISTOPHER. (*Getting it from cupboard.*) It isn't cold.
SALLY. That's all right. I'm terribly thirsty, and we've just got time before his car arrives to fetch us to lunch. (*Christopher gets a bottle and glasses from the washstand. Fritz crosses to couch.*) How are you, Fritz? (*Sits on pouffe. Christopher brings champagne to table.*)
FRITZ. I am not good. I am not good at all.
SALLY. Oh, dear, what's the trouble now?
FRITZ. I would like to tell you. Can I, please?
SALLY. Yes, of course.
FRITZ. Chris, you remember Sally's advice about me and Natalia. I attempt it. I think it goes well. And then I go again to see her, and she sends me a note. She will not see me, she will never see me again. (*Crosses to above table* R. *of Christopher. Sally turns away in embarrassment, rises and sits on couch.*) I beg, I plead. I go again. At last she see me. She tell me it is all over. (*Christopher opens the bottle and pours.*) And she shows me a note that her father has received.
SALLY. From whom?
FRITZ. It is not signed. But it say, "Herr Landauer, beware. We are going to settle the score with all you dirty Jews. We give you twenty-four hours to leave Germany. If not, you are dead men." (*Moves down to pouffe.*)
CHRISTOPHER. (*Stopping pouring.*) Good God! When was this?
FRITZ. (*Sits.*) This was last night. And she say that with that

sort of thing she cannot think now from anything else, and I am to go away and never come back. And when I try to comfort her, and tell her that it is some silly schoolboy who writes it, she scream at me that I do not understand. That I am like all the others. That her father is worried sick, and her mother is falling all the time ohnmächtig . . .

SALLY. What is that?

CHRISTOPHER. Fainting.

FRITZ. Ja, she is falling fainting, and now will I go, please. Please. Please. Please. So I go.

SALLY. (*Embarrassed.*) Well . . . (*Rises and crosses to above table* R. *of Christopher.*) Chris, isn't that champagne ready, yet?

CHRISTOPHER. (*Roused.*) Oh, yes.

SALLY. Well, let's have it. Here, Fritz. (*Gives Fritz a glass.*) Here's how.

CHRISTOPHER. How.

FRITZ. (*Sadly.*) How.

SALLY. (*Sits in chair* L. *of table.*) Oh, this is wonderful. Even warm, it is wonderful.

CHRISTOPHER. What is Herr Landauer going to do?

SALLY. I should think he is going away, isn't he?

FRITZ. (*Crosses to below* R. *of table and turns to face them.*) No, he will not go away. He wants that Natalia and her mother should go. And Natalia will not. I think her mother will go to Paris. But Natalia will stay by her father.

SALLY. If it was me, I'd fly like a bird. If I could afford it. And I'm sure they can. I mean, what is the point of staying, with that sort of thing going on?

FRITZ. I do not know. (*Drinks again, then suddenly flings his glass from him with a melodramatic gesture.*) Verfluchter Kerl! (*Buries his head in his hands.*)

SALLY. Fritz, what on earth's the matter?

CHRISTOPHER. What is it?

FRITZ. It is I. Please, can I tell you something else? Can I tell you both something?

SALLY. Yes, of course.

FRITZ. (*Sits on chair* R. *of table.*) It is something I have never told anyone in my life before. But now I must make confession. I am a Jew.

SALLY. (*Quite unperturbed.*) Well?

FRITZ. That does not surprise you?
SALLY. (*Rises, crossing to pouffe.*) I sort of had an idea you were, especially when you made so much fuss about not being. And then I forgot all about it. But so what?
FRITZ. So what? I have lied and pretended. Even to Natalia I have lied.
CHRISTOPHER. If you were so keen on getting her, I should have thought that was the very thing to tell her.
SALLY. Her parents wanted her to marry a Jew.
FRITZ. I know. I know. She has told me that. And still I could not say it. I think I wanted it even more, that no one should ever know. Even now, I cannot be one from the Landauers, and have letters like that written to me. I am ashamed from myself, but it is so. And now I have told you, and now you know me for what I am. And it is not nice. It is not nice at all. (*A long pause.*) Well, you say something, please.
SALLY. Fritz, I think you are taking it all too seriously. I mean, it is your own business.
FRITZ. I do not think it is any more. But still I cannot speak. (*Bell rings.*)
SALLY. (*Crossing to table.*) That'll be the car. Clive's car. Quick, let's have another drop of champagne. Fritz?
FRITZ. No, I do not want any more.
SALLY. Come on, it'll do you good. Here . . . (*Offers Fritz her glass. He pushes it away.*) Oh, well, have it your own way. (*Moves away to behind pouffe.*)
CHRISTOPHER. (*Touching Fritz.*) Fritz, I am terribly sorry. (*Schneider enters with a note. She gives it to Sally and goes out again. Sally puts glass down on pouffe and opens letter.*) I know it's not for me to give you any advice. I don't think I could, anyhow. But don't you think maybe you should tell Natalia that . . .
SALLY. (*Who has opened the note and read it.*) But . . . but . . . (*She cannot speak.*)
CHRISTOPHER. What is it, Sally?
SALLY. Oh, it's nothing. Look, Fritz, we've got to go out to lunch . . .
CHRISTOPHER. (*Shocked.*) But, Sally . . .
SALLY. (*Sharply, moving in to* L. *of table.*) Well, we have. And right away. Fritz, I'm not trying to get rid of you, but we do have to go.

FRITZ. Ja. Ja. Of course.
SALLY. I'm most terribly sorry. And please, please come back. Come back soon.
FRITZ. (*Rises.*) But you are going away.
SALLY. Oh . . . yes . . . Well, come tomorrow.
FRITZ. I will see. Good-bye, Sally. Good-bye, Chris. I think maybe now I go pray a little. But in what church? I do not know. (*Exit. Sally sits chair* L. *of table.*)
CHRISTOPHER. Really, Sally, that was a little cruel. Fritz really is in trouble . . .
SALLY. Yes, well, so are we. Real trouble. Read that. (*Hands Christopher the note. He crosses to above pouffe.*) Read it aloud, will you? I want to be sure I got it right.
CHRISTOPHER. (*Reading.*) "Dear Sally and Chris, I can't stick this damned town any longer. I'm off to the States. Hoping to see you sometime. Clive. These are in case I forgot anything." (*Looks in the envelope.*) Three hundred marks. (*A long pause.*) Well! (*Picks up glass and sits on pouffe.*)
SALLY. I should think you might be able to say something better than "well."
CHRISTOPHER. I said "well" when it happened. I can't think of anything else to say, now it isn't going to.
SALLY. Do you think it's true?
CHRISTOPHER. Do you want to ring up the hotel and see? See if he's gone?
SALLY. No, you do it. I don't want him to think I'm running after him.
CHRISTOPHER. I feel rather the same way.
SALLY. We could ask Fräulein Schneider to phone. (*Opens door.*) Fräulein Schneider . . . Fräulein Schneider . . .
CHRISTOPHER. (*Puts drink on table.*) What are you going to tell her?
SALLY. Nothing. Just ask her to phone. (*Sally comes back to to above chair* R. *of table. Christopher moves to above pouffe. Schneider enters. Sally goes to her.*)
SCHNEIDER. You called for me? (*Christopher sits on pouffe.*)
SALLY. (*Over-sweetly.*) Yes, Schneiderchen. Will you be a liebling, and call the Adlon Hotel, and ask for Mr. Mortimer?
SCHNEIDER. You want to speak to him?
SALLY. No, I don't. I just want you to ask for him. And if he is

there—well, say we'll be a little late for lunch. And then come and tell us. (*Kisses Schneider. Schneider goes without a word.*)
CHRISTOPHER. You know he's gone, don't you?
SALLY. (*Crosses to table and leans on it.*) I suppose I do, really. But we've got to be sure. Do you think he did it on purpose? Just to get us all steamed up, and then let us down like this?
CHRISTOPHER. I think he just got fed up
SALLY. And what about us?
CHRISTOPHER. I don't imagine he even remembered us—or not for more than a minute. I think that's the way he lives. And that he leaves every town and every set of acquaintances just that way.
SALLY. Easy come, easy go.
CHRISTOPHER. Yes.
SALLY. We were easy come, all right. (*Crosses to* R. *of Christopher.*) But, Chris, don't you think it was outrageous? I mean, really outrageous?
CHRISTOPHER. Sally, I don't think we've got too much right to have an opinion anyway, about the whole thing.
SALLY. (*Moves round pouffe to couch and sits.*) And what have we got out of it?
CHRISTOPHER. Not much. But it didn't last very long.
SALLY. I don't think we're much good as gold-diggers, are we, darling? (*Christopher and Sally begin to laugh. Schneider returns.*)
SCHNEIDER. Herr Mortimer has left, Fräulein. He has gone back to the United States.
SALLY. I see. Thank you.
CHRISTOPHER. (*Rises and comes to below* C. *of table.*) And, Fräulein Schneider, we won't be going away—after all.
SCHNEIDER. (*Overjoyed.*) Ah, Herr Issyvoo, you mean that?
CHRISTOPHER. Yes, I do.
SCHNEIDER. Oh, but that is good. (*Crosses to pouffe.*) This is wonderful. Neither of you? Not Fräulein Sally, either?
SALLY. (*Rises and crosses to below pouffe.*) No, neither of us. (*Christopher moves round above table.*)
SCHNEIDER. Then, that is a miracle. Oh, but I am happy. I am happy. (*Seizes Sally by the waist and starts to dance. They finish up in front of table.*)
SALLY. (*Releasing herself.*) Yes, I'm sure you're happy, Fräulein. But not now, please. I'd like you to leave us alone.

SCHNEIDER. (*Repentant.*) But, of course. Forgive me, Fräulein Sally. I go now. Thank you. (*Exit.*)
CHRISTOPHER. (*Crosses to* L. *of table.*) Do you want to come out and have some lunch?
SALLY. I don't think I could eat any.
CHRISTOPHER. I don't, either.
SALLY. Well, there we are. We've got three hundred marks.
CHRISTOPHER. (*Gives Sally money and crosses to above pouffe.*) What are you going to do with them?
SALLY. We'll divide them.
CHRISTOPHER. No, you take them. They were sent to you.
SALLY. (*Going to Christopher.*) They were meant for both of us. Halves, Chris. (*Halves the money.*)
CHRISTOPHER. Well, thank you.
SALLY. (*Crosses to bed and picks up négligée.*) I shall take this négligé back.
CHRISTOPHER. (*Puts parcel on floor.*) I'll take this suit back, too.
SALLY. (*Changing into mules and opening the jacket of her suit.*) And we shall have to find some work. There was a man who wrote to me the other day about a job in Frankfurt. I never answered him, because I thought we'd be gone. I'll go and see him this afternoon. (*Starting to go through her address book on small table* U. R.) He's a horrible old man, and he's always trying to go to bed with me, but I've got to make some money, somehow—I suppose. I've got his address here, somewhere.
CHRISTOPHER. I'll have to put my advertisement in the paper again. English lessons given.
SALLY. (*Finding something else.*) Oh, and there's this. (*Coming* D. C.) Do you want to earn some money, Chris?
CHRISTOPHER. You know I do. I need to. (*Puts suit box on floor.*)
SALLY. (*Pouring champagne.*) Well, there's a man who's starting a magazine. It's going to be terribly highbrow with lots of marvellous modern photographs—you know, girls' heads reflected upside down in inkpots. (*Passing drinks.*) Here, Chris. It's silly to waste it. (*Goes up to washstand with bottle, then down to table.*) Well, he wanted me to write an article in the first number on the English girl. I forgot all about it, and I haven't an idea what to say, so why don't you do it for me? I'll give you the money.

CHRISTOPHER. (*Rises, crosses up to washstand and puts glass down.*) That's wonderful. Thank you. But you must have part. (*Sits chair* L. *of table.*) How soon do you want it done?
SALLY. I should give it him in a day or two at the latest.
CHRISTOPHER. How long is it to be?
SALLY. Oh, I don't know. About *that long.* (*Gesticulates, then gets a book from small table* U. R.) Here's a dictionary, in case there are any words you can't spell.
CHRISTOPHER. (*Takes it, amused.*) Good.
SALLY. (*Her arms around his neck.*) Oh, Chris, I do like you. You're like a marvellous brother.
CHRISTOPHER. I feel the same thing. But you know, Sally, we've been delivered from something. From the Devil. I know it's disappointing, in a way . . . That's where the old plays and operas were wrong . . . There ought to be a sort of disappointment chorus at the end. But it is another chance.
SALLY. (*Sits on pouffe.*) Yes, I know. It couldn't have gone on forever. Clive wasn't the type. He'd have ditched us somewhere, and that would have been far worse.
CHRISTOPHER. It would have been worse still if he hadn't ditched us.
SALLY. He never meant to play straight with us. You're right. He was the Devil.
CHRISTOPHER. I didn't mean that. The Devil was in *us.* Sally, how about our trying to reform, and change our way of life a bit?
SALLY. What's wrong with our way of life?
CHRISTOPHER. Just about everything. Isn't it?
SALLY. (*Rises and crosses to chair* R. *of table.*) I suppose so. Not getting any work. Not even trying to. That operation. The lies I've written Mummy. The way I haven't written home at all for weeks now.
CHRISTOPHER. Me, too. Can't we reform, Sally?
SALLY. (*Sits.*) Yes, we can. I'll tell you something, Chris. Something I've just decided.
CHRISTOPHER. What's that?
SALLY. I'm sick of being a tart. I'm never going to look at another man with money, as long as I live. (*Christopher laughs.*) What's funny about that?
CHRISTOPHER. Nothing. It's a good beginning, anyway.
SALLY. What are you going to begin on?

CHRISTOPHER. I'm going to start work tomorrow morning.
SALLY. (*Carried away.*) We're both going to begin. We're going to be good. Oh, Chris, isn't it wonderful?
CHRISTOPHER. (*Rises and leans on table, smiling.*) Yes, Sally.
SALLY. (*Rises and crosses to pouffe.*) We're going to be quite, quite different people. We're even going to look wonderful, too. People will turn around and stare at us in the street, because our eyes will be shining like diamonds.
CHRISTOPHER. Diamonds—without any rings under them.
SALLY. (*Very gaily.*) And think how we'll feel in the mornings. Imagine what it will be like to wake up without coughing, or feeling even the least little bit sick.
CHRISTOPHER. We'll have appetites like wolves. Ravening wolves.
SALLY. Don't you suppose we ought to diet? Eat just nuts and things?
CHRISTOPHER. All right. And we'll give up smoking in bed . . .
SALLY. And drinking before breakfast.
CHRISTOPHER. (*Shocked.*) Sally, do you?
SALLY. (*Crosses to chair* R. *of table and kneels on it.*) We must have a timetable. What time shall we get up?
CHRISTOPHER. Eight o'clock.
SALLY. Half-past seven.
CHRISTOPHER. All right.
SALLY. We shall take cold baths. You have yours first.
CHRISTOPHER. And do exercises.
SALLY. Then we'll have breakfast together, and talk German. Nothing but German.
CHRISTOPHER. Ja. Jawohl.
SALLY. (*Rises and crosses to* L. *of Christopher.*) Then we should study something. Do you think we could learn a useful trade?
CHRISTOPHER. We'll weave from eight-thirty to nine. And then spend an hour making small, hand-painted boxes.
SALLY. (*Laughing hard.*) And then it'll be time for you to start your novel, while I practise interpretive dancing. You know, with shawls and things . . . (*Gets towel from rack and dances with it.*)
CHRISTOPHER. Sally, joking aside. You are serious about all this, aren't you?
SALLY. (*Drops towel on chair.*) Of course I am. Terribly serious.

(*Gets the address book from table and crosses to couch with it.*) I'm going to start ringing up everyone I know.
CHRISTOPHER. What for?
SALLY. To see what's going on. (*Lies on couch.*) And then, one decent piece of luck . . .
CHRISTOPHER. (*Sits on pouffe. Urgently.*) Oh, no, Sally. That isn't what we need. A piece of good luck today—a piece of bad luck tomorrow—always at the mercy of *things* again . . .
SALLY. One *is*. That's life. It's all accident.
CHRISTOPHER. (*As before.*) Accidents are only the result of things one's done. Things that one is.
SALLY. Why, I could go to a party tonight, and I could meet the most wonderful man, who'd make all the difference to my whole life, and my career . . . (*She breaks off, looking at him.*) What's the matter? Why do you look like that?
CHRISTOPHER. (*Slowly.*) Sally, you weren't serious. You didn't mean a word of it.
SALLY. Yes, I did. I meant every word. I'm going to be quite different. But there's no reason why I shouldn't go out. I don't have to shut myself up in prison. (*Rises.*) That isn't what you want, is it?
CHRISTOPHER. (*Rises.*) No, Sally, of course not. But . . .
SALLY. (*Angrily.*) Well, then, stop looking so disapproving. You're almost as bad as my mother. She never stopped nagging at me. That's why I had to lie to her. I always lie to people, or run away from them if they won't accept me as I am.
CHRISTOPHER. I know you do, Sally.
SALLY. (*Putting on an act.*) I think I'm really rather a strange and extraordinary person, Chris. (*Pause.*) What's the matter? You laughed at me the first time I told you that. Can't you laugh now? Come on. (*Sally starts to laugh, not too brightly. He starts a moment later, still more feebly. The laughter dies. She tries again, it fails. They move slowly away from each other.*)

CURTAIN

ACT III

SCENE 1

Two days later. The room is untidy. A half-used coffee tray is on the table with a glass of brandy. The bed is unmade and clothes are strewn around the room. Sofa and table are back as in Act I. Sally's makeup is on the table.

Schneider is picking up a pair of pants from behind couch as the curtain rises. She crosses to in front of couch, picks up shoes and puts them down in front of chair U. R. *There is a knock on the door.*

CHRISTOPHER. (*Off.*) Sally, may I come in?
SCHNEIDER. Come in, Herr Issyvoo. (*Christopher comes in.*) Fräulein Sally is telephoning.
CHRISTOPHER. She's up very late.
SCHNEIDER. She was in very late last night.
CHRISTOPHER. I left a manuscript in here for her yesterday afternoon.
SCHNEIDER. (*Picks up Sally's hat and jacket from couch and skirt from floor* R. *of table.*) She did not come back until almost six this morning. I think maybe she drank a little too much. And she had only half her chocolate this morning, and some brandy too. It is not good so early. (*Christopher crosses up to behind couch. Sally enters, and crosses to table. She is wearing a robe, and looks hung-over. She is smoking.*)
SALLY. Oh, hello, Chris.
CHRISTOPHER. Hello, Sally.
SALLY. Leave all that stuff for now, Fräulein. I'm going to wear it. I'm going out quite soon. You can do the room then. (*Schneider puts clothes on chair below washstand.*)
SCHNEIDER. Very good, Fräulein. (*Exit. Sally drinks brandy.*)
CHRISTOPHER. I haven't seen you for a day and a half.

SALLY. I know. I've missed you, Chris. (*Sits in chair above table.*)
CHRISTOPHER. (*Crossing to* R. *of her.*) I've missed you, too. I say, you don't look too well this morning.
SALLY. I've got a terrible hangover.
CHRISTOPHER. What have you been up to?
SALLY. Oh, not *that.*
CHRISTOPHER. I wasn't thinking of that!
SALLY. But we never stopped going around. And then I got drunk and sentimental the first night, and I telephoned Mummy in London.
CHRISTOPHER. (*Lying on couch.*) Good God, what for?
SALLY. I suddenly felt like it. But we had the most awful connection, and I couldn't hear a word. And last night was worse. We went to the most boring places. (*Moves to couch and sits on it by Christopher.*) Oh, Chris, I need someone to stop me. I really do. I wish I'd stayed home with you.
CHRISTOPHER. Well, thank you, Sally.
SALLY. But you're awfully nice to come back to.
CHRISTOPHER. You're awfully nice to have back. I say, that sounds like a popular song.
SALLY. Oh, it does. Maybe we could write it together and make a fortune. (*Improvises a tune.*) "You're awfully nice to come back to."
CHRISTOPHER. (*Doing the same.*) "You're awfully nice to have back."
SALLY.
CHRISTOPHER. } (*Singing together.*) { "You're awfully nice to come back to . . ." (*They laugh.*)
SALLY. (*Her arms around Christopher.*) I do think we belong together. Much more than if we'd ever had an affair. That little quarrel we had didn't mean anything, did it? (*Rises and goes to screen for stockings and shoes.*)
CHRISTOPHER. I don't think two people can live as close as we do, and not have them.
SALLY. (*Comes back to couch and sits* L. *end of it.*) But it was that that sent me out on that idiotic binge.
CHRISTOPHER. (*Pause.*) Did you read the article I left you?
SALLY. The what, dear?
CHRISTOPHER. My article.
SALLY. (*Vaguely.*) Oh, yes, I—looked at it.

CHRISTOPHER. Well?
SALLY. (*Too brightly.*) I'm terribly sorry, Chris. But it won't do.
CHRISTOPHER. Why, what's wrong with it? (*Goes to small table* U. R. *and picks up typescript.*)
SALLY. It's not nearly snappy enough.
CHRISTOPHER. Snappy? (*Down to pouffe.*)
SALLY. But it's all right, Christopher. I've got someone else to do it. (*Polishes her shoes on her dressing gown.*)
CHRISTOPHER? Oh? Who?
SALLY. Kurt Rosenthal. I called him this morning.
CHRISTOPHER. Who's he?
SALLY. (*Turns to Christopher.*) Really, Chris, I thought you took an interest in the cinema. He's miles the best young scenario writer. He earns pots of money.
CHRISTOPHER. Then why's he doing this?
SALLY. As a favor to me. He said he'd dictate it while he's shaving, and send it round to the editor's flat.
CHRISTOPHER. Well, journalism isn't really in my line. But I think you might have let me know. (*Sits on pouffe.*)
SALLY. (*Rises and crosses behind him.*) I didn't think you'd want to be bothered.
CHRISTOPHER. And *he* would? (*Sally takes off and drops dressing gown on couch. Goes up to chair for skirt.*)
SALLY. (*Starting to dress.*) He doesn't make such a fuss about writing as you do. He's writing a novel in his spare time. He's so terribly busy, he can only dictate it while he's having a bath. (*Does skirt up.*)
CHRISTOPHER. (*Rises and crosses up to behind couch. Bitterly.*) I bet that makes it wonderful. Of course it depends how many baths he takes.
SALLY. He read me the first few chapters. Honestly, I think it's the best novel I've ever read.
CHRISTOPHER. (*Drops article on couch.*) But that doesn't add up to very many, does it? (*Sally comes down to table for cigarette, then goes to washstand and brushes hair.*)
SALLY. (*Her tone sharpening.*) He's the kind of author I really admire. And he's not stuck up, either. Not like one of these young men who, because they've written one book, start talking about art, and imagining they're the most wonderful authors in the world.

CHRISTOPHER. (*In to her.*) Just who are you talking about, Sally?
SALLY. (*Brushing her hair.*) Well, you do, Chris. You know you do. And it's silly to get jealous.
CHRISTOPHER. (*Angrily.*) Jealous? Who's jealous?
SALLY. There's no need to get upset, either. (*Puts hat on and crosses down to him.*)
CHRISTOPHER. (*Furious.*) I am not upset. You don't like my article. All right, you needn't go on about it. I can't think why I expected you to; or your rich, successful friends either, from whom you seem to have got all this stuff about me.
SALLY. (*Equally angry.*) Would you like to know what my friends said about you?
CHRISTOPHER. No, I wouldn't.
SALLY. Well, I'll tell you. They said you were ruining me. That I'd lost all my sparkle and my effervescence. And that it was all due to you. I've let you eat me up, just sitting here, pouring myself into you.
CHRISTOPHER. Oh, is that what you've been doing?
SALLY. It's all you want. You're like a vampire. If you don't have someone around you, you sit about in bars waiting to devour someone. (*Sits in chair above table.*)
CHRISTOPHER. Your friends said that?
SALLY. My friends are a lot better than the tatty people you run around with. (*Spits into mascara and does her eyelashes.*) All your friends seem to be interested in, is just flopping into bed.
CHRISTOPHER. (*In to her.*) And since when have you had anything against bed?
SALLY. I haven't anything. So long as it leads somewhere.
CHRISTOPHER. You mean not just for the fun of it. (*Moves away.*)
SALLY. That's disgusting. That's like animals. (*Rises and goes to chair for jacket which she puts on, then comes back to him.*) But, you know, Chris. I'll tell you something. I've outgrown you.
CHRISTOPHER. (*Turns to her.*) You've *what?*
SALLY. I've gone beyond you. I'd better move away from here.
CHRISTOPHER. All right. When?
SALLY. The sooner the better, I should think.
CHRISTOPHER. That's fine with me.
SALLY. Good.

CHRISTOPHER. So, this is the end for us?
SALLY. (*Picks up handbag from table and starts moving to door.*) Yes. If you want it that way. We'll probably bump into each other somewhere, sometime, I expect.
CHRISTOPHER. Well, call me sometime, and ask me around for a cocktail.
SALLY. (*Pausing at door.*) I never know whether you're being serious, or not.
CHRISTOPHER. Try it and find out, if your friends will spare you the time.
SALLY. (*Throwing it at him.*) You know, you make me sick. Good-bye, Chris. (*Goes out, slamming door.*)
CHRISTOPHER. (*Moves towards door.*) What a little bitch she is! Well, I've always known that from the start. No, that's not true. I've flattered myself she was fond of me. Nothing would please me better than to see her whipped. Really whipped. Not that I care a curse what she thinks of my article . . . (*Picks it up.*) Well, not much. My literary conceit is proof against anything she could say. (*Comes down to table and throws it in waste basket.*) It's her criticism of myself. The awful, sexual flair women have for taking the stuffing out of men. It's no good telling myself that Sally had the vocabulary and mind of a twelve-year-old schoolgirl . . . I mismanaged our interview, right from the beginning. I should have been wonderful, convincing, fatherly, mature. I made the one fatal mistake. I let her see I was jealous. Vulgarly jealous. I feel prickly all over with shame. Friends, indeed! Well, I certainly won't see her again, after all this. Never. Never! (*Sally returns, very shattered.*)
SALLY. Chris, something awful's happened. Guess who I met on the stairs. I met Mummy.
CHRISTOPHER. What mummy?
SALLY. Mine.
CHRISTOPHER. I thought you said she was in London.
SALLY. (*Crosses to couch and puts bag down.*) She was. But that call of mine upset her. I suppose I did sound a bit drunk. Anyway, she jumped to conclusions, and into an aeroplane. Chris, you're going to have to do something for me. I've been writing her now and then . . . I mean, they do send me money from time to time. I've never had the nerve to tell you, but I sort of gave

her to understand, when I first moved in here, that we were engaged.

CHRISTOPHER. That who was engaged?

SALLY. You and I. To be married.

CHRISTOPHER. Sally, you didn't!

SALLY. (*Picks up dressing gown and slippers.*) Well, I needed someone who sounded like a good, steady influence, and you were the best I could think of. She's in the sitting-room. I told her this place was all untidy, but she'll be in in a minute. Oh, and her name isn't Mrs. Bowles. It's Mrs. Watson-Courtneidge. That's my real name. Only you can't imagine the Germans pronouncing it.

CHRISTOPHER. And I'm supposed to stand by and pretend? Oh, no, Sally. (*Sally drops dressing gown and slippers on floor.*)

SALLY. Chris, you've got to. (*In to Christopher.*) You owe it to me.

CHRISTOPHER. For what? For letting me eat you up? I'm sorry. And I'm going to my room. (*Starts to go.*)

SALLY. (*Running round back of couch and getting in his way.*) If you don't, I'll tell her the most awful things about you.

CHRISTOPHER. I'm afraid I don't care. Tell her what you like.

SALLY. (*Pleading and pushing Christopher back into the room.*) Chris, you can't do this to me.

CHRISTOPHER. After the things you just said to me? That I made you sick.

SALLY. That was just an expression.

CHRISTOPHER. No, Sally. We're through. Quite through.

SALLY. Well, we still can be, after she goes home. Only, help me keep her happy. Don't believe everything I said at first. She isn't easy. Please, darling. Please! (*Throws her arms round Christopher. Christopher struggles to disengage himself. Then Mrs. Watson-Courtneidge comes in. She is a middle-aged English lady, in tweeds. She carries a cloak. She shuts the door.*)

MRS. WATSON. (*Catching sight of the embrace.*) Excuse me.

SALLY. (*Extricating herself.*) Oh . . .

MRS. WATSON. (*Coming down to* R. *of pouffe.*) I hope this is Mr. Isherwood.

SALLY. Yes, Christopher.

MRS. WATSON. I'm Mummy.

CHRISTOPHER. I imagined that.

MRS WATSON. Well—don't I deserve a kiss, too?

CHRISTOPHER. (*As Sally looks pleadingly at him.*) Oh—yes, of course. (*Christopher goes to Mrs. Watson and a kiss is performed.*)
MRS. WATSON. You're not a bit like I imagined you.
CHRISTOPHER. Oh, really. How did you imagine me?
MRS. WATSON. Oh, quite different. (*Crosses to table.*) So this is your room, Sally. Yes, I can see why you said it was untidy.
SALLY. (*Picks up dressing gown and puts it on the bed.*) I got up very late this morning. Fräulein Schneider hasn't really had time to do it.
MRS. WATSON. I don't imagine she does it very well at the best of times. I've just been having a little talk to her. I can't say I like her very much. And why does she sleep in the sitting-room?
CHRISTOPHER. (*Moving to head of couch.*) So that she can watch the corner.
MRS. WATSON. And what happens on the corner? (*Goes to above table, puts cloak down on chair and handbag on table.*)
CHRISTOPHER. Oh—*that!*
SALLY. Chris!
MRS. WATSON. I beg your pardon?
CHRISTOPHER. (*Vaguely.*) This and that.
MRS. WATSON. I should think she'd be much better occupied looking after . . . (*Dusting the table with her fingers.*) that and this! (*Picks up the brandy glass.*) Sally, you haven't been drinking brandy, I hope.
SALLY. That's Chris's glass.
MRS. WATSON. On *your* breakfast tray? (*Steps towards Christopher.*) Where do you live, Mr. Isherwood?
CHRISTOPHER. Just across the hall.
MRS. WATSON. (*Dryly.*) How convenient!
SALLY. (*Steps towards Mrs. Watson.*) What do you mean by that, Mummy?
MRS. WATSON. Sally, dear, I'm not asking for details. There are things one doesn't choose to know. But tell me, you two, when are you getting married?
SALLY. I don't know, Mummy. We're happy as—we are. Aren't we, Chris? (*Sits* L. *end of couch.*)
CHRISTOPHER. (*Grimly.*) Just as we are.
MRS. WATSON. (*Takes gloves off and moves slightly* U. S.) I can well believe it. But sooner or later, these things have to be—

well, shall we say?—tidied up. There are some questions I would like to ask you, Mr. Isherwood.
CHRISTOPHER. (*Moving round to behind couch.*) Yes?
MRS. WATSON. I've read your book.
CHRISTOPHER. Oh, really?
MRS. WATSON. After Sally wrote me the title, I got it from the library—with a good deal of trouble. It's an odd book. Was it a success?
CHRISTOPHER. No. Not really.
MRS. WATSON. That doesn't altogether surprise me. I take it you don't live on your writing?
CHRISTOPHER. No. Hardly. (*Warningly.*) Sally!
MRS. WATSON. What do you live on?
CHRISTOPHER. I teach English.
MRS. WATSON. And is that sufficient?
CHRISTOPHER. I get by.
MRS. WATSON. Can two get by?
CHRISTOPHER. I'm inclined to doubt it. (*As before, but more so.*) Sally!
MRS. WATSON. (*Crosses to table, puts gloves down and takes handkerchief from handbag.*) Well, that is not my concern. That will be Sally's father's.
CHRISTOPHER. (*Getting no response from Sally.*) Well, now if you'll excuse me, Sally . . . (*Starts to go.*)
MRS. WATSON. Are you not lunching with us?
SALLY. Yes, of course he is. (*Going to Christopher.*)
CHRISTOPHER. Sally, I can't.
SALLY. Yes, you can. You were lunching with me.
CHRISTOPHER. Look, I think there's something we ought to clear up. (*Christopher comes down to below couch. Sally follows him.*)
SALLY. *No!*
MRS. WATSON. What is that? (*Silence a moment. Then Christopher gives way.*)
CHRISTOPHER. I haven't got any decent clothes.
MRS. WATSON. My dear Mr. Isherwood, it's not your clothes we want, it's your company. I know all about your background. Anything you wear will be all right, so long as it is clean.
CHRISTOPHER. Well, that's part of the point.

SALLY. (*Pushing him out.*) Go and change, Chris. We'll wait here for you.
CHRISTOPHER. (*After a look at her.*) I won't be a minute. (*Exit.*)
MRS. WATSON. He's an odd young man, Sally.
SALLY. Oh, I don't know, Mummy.
MRS. WATSON. (*Going to* L. *of Sally.*) Tell me, that strange telephone call of yours—how much was Mr. Isherwood involved in it?
SALLY. Involved?
MRS. WATSON. Had you had a few too many cocktails because of some, well, little quarrel with him?
SALLY. Oh, no, Mummy. Chris and I never quarrel.
MRS. WATSON. Well, in any case, I think you two have been together quite long enough for the moment. (*Moves away to table.*) You had better move into the hotel with me.
SALLY. (*Protesting.*) No, Mummy, I . . . (*Goes towards Mrs. Watson.*)
MRS. WATSON. Sally, don't answer back. (*Sally sits on couch.*) You always answer back. I've begun to realize that things are a little more complicated than I had imagined. (*Goes to above couch* L. *of Sally.*) Hasn't Mr. Isherwood suggested any date for your wedding?
SALLY. No, Mummy, I don't think he has.
MRS. WATSON. I'm not suggesting he will let you down. He's a gentleman. That's one comfort. But . . .
SALLY. (*Kneeling on couch, urgently.*) Mummy, you've got entirely the wrong idea about Chris and me. We aren't . . .
MRS. WATSON. (*Interrupting.*) Sally, that is something you might have had to say to your grandmother. You don't have to say it to me.
SALLY. But, Mummy . . .
MRS. WATSON. (*As before.*) Mummy's quite broad-minded. (*Goes to table, puts handkerchief in bag and gets out smelling salts.*)
SALLY. (*Giving way.*) Well, all right, but don't rush him. Don't try and force him, or anything.
MRS. WATSON. Trust Mummy! I see you still have that picture. You had that in the nursery. "The Kitten's Awakening." I'm glad

you still have that. (*Sits* R. *of Sally.*) The old things are still the best, after all, aren't they?
SALLY. (*Subdued.*) Yes, Mummy.
MRS. WATSON. (*Embracing Sally.*) We must get you back to them.

CURTAIN

ACT III

SCENE 2

The same. Afternoon. About three days later.
Fritz is on stage lying on couch reading a newspaper and smoking. Schneider is pouring coffee for him. The old pictures are back on the walls. The room is again as in Scene 1.

SCHNEIDER. (*At table.*) He is always back around this time, Herr Wendel. You cannot have to wait long. (*Goes to Fritz with coffee.*)
FRITZ. Danke. I am glad that Christopher could move back into this room again. Will he stay on here?
SCHNEIDER. Oh, I hope. He is doing better now. Starting new lessons. It is true they are almost all to the Jews, but even so there is at least some good that comes from them that way. (*Fritz does not answer.*) Is it true, Herr Wendel, that they will take the money away from the Jews, and drive them all out?
FRITZ. I have no idea. (*Rises and puts cup down on table.*)
SCHNEIDER. It would be a good thing. (*To* R. *of Fritz.*) Do you not agree with me?
FRITZ. I do not really know.
SCHNEIDER. But you must know, Herr Wendel. That is what the speakers all say. Everyone must know, and everyone must agree and only then can Germany be saved. (*Voices heard off stage. Schneider goes to door. Fritz to above couch.*)
CHRISTOPHER. (*Off.*) Go right in there, Natalia. Are you sure you're all right?
NATALIA. (*Off.*) Oh, yes, I thank you. I am all right.
CHRISTOPHER. (*Off.*) And then come to my room. It's the old

room. (*Christopher comes in. He is a little more messed up than usual. He crosses to Fritz and Schneider goes out.*) Oh, hello, Fritz. I didn't know you were here.
FRITZ. Was that Natalia's voice I heard outside?
CHRISTOPHER. Yes, she's gone to the bathroom. I must wash my hands. (*Takes jacket off and hangs it over chair by washstand.*)
FRITZ. What is the matter?
CHRISTOPHER. There was a bit of trouble. (*Pours water into the basin.*)
FRITZ. But what is it all about?
CHRISTOPHER. (*Washing his hands.*) I was walking with Natalia after her lesson. We ran into a bunch of toughs. Nazis, of course. They were holding a street meeting. And Natalia insisted on joining in.
FRITZ. Joining in?
CHRISTOPHER. Yes, she got quite fierce. She made a speech. She was almost like Joan of Arc. I was quite astonished.
FRITZ. She is wonderful, that girl.
CHRISTOPHER. And she was hit in the face with a stone.
FRITZ. Um Gotteswillen.
CHRISTOPHER. It wasn't serious. At least, I don't think it was. I wanted her to go to a doctor, but she wouldn't. I think she is a bit shaken, that's all.
FRITZ. It is better perhaps if your landlady does not see her. (*Goes to table and puts cigarette out.*)
CHRISTOPHER. Why? (*Getting tin of plaster dressings out of cupboard.*)
FRITZ. She is not very partial to the Jews, your landlady. (*Crosses to couch and sits.*)
CHRISTOPHER. Yes, I know. But she doesn't know what she is talking about. (*Comes down to table with dressings.*)
FRITZ. She knows as much as most people.
CHRISTOPHER. And that is the tragedy. (*Takes a series of dressings, and starts to put them on his hands rather excessively.*)
FRITZ. What is wrong with your hands? Were you in it, too?
CHRISTOPHER. Well, after Natalia started, I couldn't really keep out of it. Trying to get her away.
FRITZ. Natalia should not stay here.
CHRISTOPHER. She'll stay as long as her father stays.

FRITZ. She would go if she married.
CHRISTOPHER. I doubt that.
FRITZ. (*Urgently.*) But she ought to go! Christopher, I know now I am in love with Natalia. I have not seen her, but I am in love with her. (*Rises and goes to* R. *of Christopher. Natalia enters and crosses to* R. *of couch. There is a small scar, newly washed, on her face. Fritz steps forward.*)
NATALIA. So, Christopher, I think now . . . (*Sees Fritz, and stops.*) Oh, Fritz.
FRITZ. Ja, Natalia.
NATALIA. Christopher did not tell me you were here.
FRITZ. He did not know.
CHRISTOPHER. Let me give you some brandy, Natalia.
NATALIA. I do not think so. (*Sits on couch.*)
CHRISTOPHER. Yes, but I do think so. You need something. And it's quite good brandy. It's part of—quite a good loot. I'm going to have some. (*Goes to cupboard, gets brandy and glasses and brings them down to table.*)
FRITZ. (*To Natalia.*) Please, may I see your face?
NATALIA. (*Turning.*) There is nothing there.
FRITZ. (*Kneeling.*) I would like to see, please. It is clean? You have washed it? You have washed it thoroughly?
NATALIA. I have washed it thoroughly.
CHRISTOPHER. Would you like to put a Band-Aid on?
NATALIA. On my face? (*Fritz crosses to table.*)
CHRISTOPHER. I think you should. You can get blood poisoning.
NATALIA. And a bandage will help that?
CHRISTOPHER. (*Going to cupboard.*) I have some iodine. I can put that on for you.
NATALIA. Not on my face, I thank you. (*Fritz goes back to Natalia and kneels* R. *of her, leaving glass on couch as he goes.*)
FRITZ. You let me put one of these on. Just a very small one. Like so. (*Holds one up.*)
NATALIA. (*Touched, but unwilling to show it.*) I can put it on myself. (*Christopher returns to table with iodine.*)
FRITZ. I know, but let me do it, please. You drink your brandy, and let me do it. (*Starts to do so.*)
CHRISTOPHER. (*Looking at his hands.*) You know, I wonder if

I shouldn't take these Band-Aids off, and put on some iodine. I could get gangrene.

NATALIA. No, Christopher, you could not.

CHRISTOPHER. You never know. Then they amputate your hands. And you can't write or type any more. (*Tears off the dressings and paints on iodine.*)

FRITZ. (*Finishing his job.*) There. (*Seems to feel a little faint.*) Now I take some brandy. (*Fritz goes to table. He and Natalia gulp some brandy, hastily.*)

NATALIA. And now I think I go home. (*Turns to go.*)

FRITZ. You let me take you, please. (*Crosses to* C.)

NATALIA. My dear young man, I . . .

FRITZ. (*Finishing for her.*) I am not yet sixty years old, and I can go home unmolested.

NATALIA. I prefer that I go alone.

FRITZ. I would like that you let me take you.

NATALIA. (*Crossing to Fritz.*) And if we run into another of these street riots?

FRITZ. I would still like to take you. (*Christopher raises his head. The two men exchange glances. Fritz nods very gently and puts down glass on table.*) I tell it now.

CHRISTOPHER. Let him take you, Natalia. I would feel better.

NATALIA. Very well. I see you tomorrow, Christopher. At the usual hour. Yes? (*Fritz goes to Natalia.*)

CHRISTOPHER. Yes, of course. Good-bye, Natalia. I admired you very much this afternoon.

FRITZ. I, too.

NATALIA. I cannot see why. Come. (*She goes out with Fritz. Christopher looks after them, then picks up the box of dressings and the iodine. He crosses couch, finishes Natalia's brandy and resumes his painting.*)

CHRISTOPHER. It doesn't look too good. (*Splashes on some more iodine. Schneider comes in and crosses to table.*)

SCHNEIDER. I take the coffee tray. What is with your hands, Herr Issyvoo?

CHRISTOPHER. I think they may be poisoned.

SCHNEIDER. But how did you come to hurt them?

CHRISTOPHER. It was in a street riot.

SCHNEIDER. An anti-Jewish riot?

CHRISTOPHER. Yes.

SCHNEIDER. And you were attacking the Jews.
CHRISTOPHER. No, I was defending them.
SCHNEIDER. But that is not right, Herr Issyvoo. The Jews are at the bottom of all the trouble.
CHRISTOPHER. (*Crosses to table with dressings and iodine and puts them down. Sharply.*) Fräulein Schneider, I think I've heard enough of that this afternoon. Let's not talk about it any more.
SCHNEIDER. But that is wrong, Herr Issyvoo. We must all talk about it. That is what the speakers say. Germany must come first.
CHRISTOPHER. (*Turning angrily.*) And what does that mean? How can any country come first that does things like that? Suppose I push this in your face. (*Thrusts his fist near Schneider's face, and she retreats.*) Because Germany must come first—and I'm strong enough to do it, and to hurt you? What does that prove?
SCHNEIDER. But, Herr Issyvoo . . .
CHRISTOPHER. I've always been fond of you. Now I'm ashamed of you. And everything you say is horrible and dangerous and abominable. And now please go away. (*Turns and moves away to table.*)
SCHNEIDER. (*Angrily.*) You will see, Herr Issyvoo. You will see. (*Bell rings.*)
CHRISTOPHER. I know that talking like this makes me almost as bad as you. Or perhaps worse. Because I've got intelligence, I hope, and you've just been listening to things. Now go and answer the bell. (*Schneider goes. Christopher cries in exasperation to himself and moves to* U. C. *of couch.*) God, what is one supposed to do? (*Examines his hands again.*) I wonder if I've broken anything. It feels awfully loose. (*Flexes his thumb.*) Ought that to move like that, or oughtn't it? (*Sally comes in. She wears the cloak her mother was carrying in the previous scene.*)
SALLY. Hello, Chris.
CHRISTOPHER. Well, fancy seeing you again, without your mother. (*Mrs. Watson-Courtneidge comes in.*) Oh, hello, Mrs. Watson-Courtneidge!
MRS. WATSON. Good afternoon, Christopher. (*Crossing to Sally's* R.)
CHRISTOPHER. And how are things with you two?
MRS. WATSON. They're very well. Sally has been making me very happy.

CHRISTOPHER. I see you've dressed her up in your clothes.
SALLY. (*Defensively.*) What's wrong with that? Mother's got very good taste.
CHRISTOPHER. But it's hardly *your* taste, is it?
MRS. WATSON. (*Over to couch and lifting the glass.*) Brandy again?
CHRISTOPHER. (*Defiantly.*) Yes. (*Goes to Mrs. Watson and takes glass from her.*)
MRS. WATSON. I see. What's the matter with your hands? (*Christopher goes to table and puts glass down.*)
CHRISTOPHER. I hurt them. I was in a fight.
SALLY. (*Crosses to above* L. *of couch.*) Good gracious, you! What was the fight about?
CHRISTOPHER. Jews.
MRS. WATSON. Why were you fighting about *them*?
CHRISTOPHER. I don't like seeing people being pushed around. (*To Sally.*) Or made to pretend they're what they're not.
MRS. WATSON. Oh, I see. (*Sits on couch.*) Well, now, Christopher, there's something I want to tell you. I'm taking Sally home.
CHRISTOPHER. Oh? And what do *you* say about that, Sally?
SALLY. (*Kneeling on couch* L. *of Mrs. Watson.*) Mummy's quite right, Chris. She really is. I ought to go home. To my past, and my roots and things. They're very important to a girl.
CHRISTOPHER. Sally, don't. Don't let her!
SALLY. Let her what?
CHRISTOPHER. You're disappearing, right in front of my eyes.
MRS. WATSON. I hope the girl you knew *is* disappearing. I want you to come, too, Christopher. Then you can meet Sally's father, and, if he approves of you, he will find you a job of some sort. Then you can be married from our house at the end of next month. That will give me time to arrange Sally's trousseau.
CHRISTOPHER. Look, Sally, haven't you told your mother yet?
SALLY. (*Miserably.*) No, not yet.
MRS. WATSON. Told me what?
CHRISTOPHER. Sally, I think you should.
SALLY. (*Desperately.*) No, Chris, not now. (*Crosses to Christopher.*)
CHRISTOPHER. Yes, now. (*Crosses below Sally to* L. *of couch.*) Mrs. Courtneidge, there's something I have to tell you. Sally and

I are no longer engaged. She sent me a note this morning, to break it off.

MRS. WATSON. Sally, you never told me.

SALLY. (*Very relieved.*) I wanted to speak to Chris first.

MRS. WATSON. This is all a little sudden.

CHRISTOPHER. I don't think it's very sudden, really. We had a sort of quarrel the morning you arrived, and we never really made it up since.

MRS. WATSON. I thought you never quarrelled.

CHRISTOPHER. Who said that?

MRS. WATSON. Sally did. Are you sure about this, Sally?

SALLY. (*Crosses to pouffe and sits.*) Well, yes, Mummy, as a matter of fact I am. I don't think Chris and I are really suited to each other.

MRS. WATSON. Neither do I. But I never hoped that you would realize it. Well, this alters everything. (*Rises.*) I will not expect *you* to come back to England, Christopher.

CHRISTOPHER. Good.

MRS. WATSON. (*Going to Sally and putting her arm round her.*) But I'm very glad that Sally has been able to see the truth for herself. I was afraid she had changed almost too much. That *you* had changed her.

SALLY. (*To Christopher.*) See?

MRS. WATSON. (*Crosses to couch.*) Sally has been very good about you, Christopher. She has continued to deny everything that I am absolutely sure has taken place. I think that shows a very fine character.

CHRISTOPHER. No doubt that was due to *your* influence.

MRS. WATSON. Perhaps you'll forgive me if I say a few things to you, Christopher. (*Sits.*) I think someone should say them, and Sally's father isn't here to do so. Perhaps that's lucky for you. He's not a patient man, and he adores Sally. I know he'd think that anyone who'd harmed her richly deserved a sound horse-whipping.

CHRISTOPHER. (*Coming towards Mrs. Watson.*) Now, listen, Mrs. Courtneidge . . .

MRS. WATSON. I have no intention of listening to you, Mr. Isherwood. Sally has done quite enough of that, already. She's a very sweet, simple girl, but she's far too easily influenced.

CHRISTOPHER. Look, do we have to go into all this?

MRS. WATSON. (*Sharply.*) Yes, I think we do. It's people like

you who are ruining the world. Unprincipled drifters who call themselves authors, never write a word, and then vote Labor on the slightest provocation. You live in foreign countries, and you let yourself get involved in obscure political issues that are no concern of yours . . .
SALLY. (*Rises, suddenly.*) Yes, they are.
MRS. WATSON. (*Surprised.*) Sally!
SALLY. (*Coming in to* R. *of couch.*) Some sort of principles are, and I'm very glad to see he has some, and that there is something he is willing to fight for, instead of just sitting around.
CHRISTOPHER. Now, Sally, wait a minute . . .
SALLY. I know. I've told you a lot of the same things, myself. But I don't like to hear her say them. Certainly not to you. You don't know Chris. You don't understand him. He's a very fine person. He's been wonderful to me. He has. He's done a lot for me, and he's tried to do more. And he's an artist. Well—potentially. All artists need time. He's going to write a wonderful book one day, that'll sell millions of copies, or a lot of short stories all about Germany or something, which will tell the world wonderful things about life and people and everything—and then you'll feel very silly for the things you've just said. (*Turns away.*)
MRS. WATSON. I thought you'd just broken off your engagement.
SALLY. (*Turns to Mrs. Watson.*) Yes, I have. But I'm not going to stand here and let you nag at him like that. He doesn't chase around after horrible influential people, and I bet he wouldn't take a job from Daddy if he offered him one. He's got too much pride. And character. It just wants—working up, that's all. And now let's go. (*Goes to door and stands by it.*)
MRS. WATSON. (*Staggered.*) Well . . . (*Rises.*) I'll say goodbye, Christopher. We shall be leaving tomorrow, or the next day. I don't imagine that we'll meet again. And I would prefer that you and Sally did not see each other again, either. Shall we go, Sally? (*Moves to door and goes out.*)
SALLY. Yes, Mummy. (*Follows, shutting door without looking at Christopher.*)
CHRISTOPHER. Well. Really? (*The outside door slams. He goes to the table, and the brandy bottle, then stops.*) No, I won't. I *will* have some principles!

CURTAIN

ACT III

SCENE 3

Three days later. Evening.
A large trunk is open in the middle of the floor. Christopher is putting things into it and sorting others from the closet. He brings four shirts from cupboard to behind couch.

CHRISTOPHER. Where did I ever get all these things? This shirt —I can't possibly have bought it. No, I didn't, of course, I remember. It was at that party at the Lithuanian sculptor's, where a whole bottle of crème-de-menthe got spilled over mine. (*Starts putting them in trunk.*) These are Clive's silk ones. I don't suppose I'll ever wear them, but you never know, they are the best silk. This pair of pants. No, really, they're too far gone. Out! (*Throws them away in waste basket and closes trunk. Enter Sally. She is dressed as in the first scene. She comes to couch and puts bag and cloak down.*)
SALLY. Chris!
CHRISTOPHER. Sally! I thought you'd gone. I thought you'd gone home.
SALLY. No. Mummy left this morning.
CHRISTOPHER. And you're not going?
SALLY. Not home. Oh, Chris, it was ghastly getting rid of Mummy. But I knew I had to, after that scene here.
CHRISTOPHER. How did you do it?
SALLY. (*Kneeling on couch, giggling.*) I did something awful. I got a friend in London to send her an anonymous telegram telling her Daddy was having an affair. That sent her off in a mad whirl. But Daddy will forgive me. Besides, it's probably true—and I don't blame him. I told Mummy I'd follow her when I got some business settled. And something will turn up to stop it. It always does, for me. I'm all right, Chris. (*Rises and goes to Christopher.*) I'm back again.
CHRISTOPHER. (*Smiling.*) Yes, I can see you are.

SALLY. Is there anything to drink?
CHRISTOPHER. There's just a little gin, that's all. (*Goes up to washstand.*)
SALLY. I'd love a little gin. In a tooth glass. Flavored with peppermint. Where are you off to? (*Sits on the trunk.*)
CHRISTOPHER. I *am* going home.
SALLY. When?
CHRISTOPHER. (*Coming down to Sally with drink.*) Tomorrow night. I'm going to Fritz and Natalia's wedding in the afternoon.
SALLY. Wedding? How did that happen?
CHRISTOPHER. (*Sits* L. *of Sally.*) Fritz told Natalia about himself, and that did it. And now he doesn't have to pretend any more. Come with me, Sally. They'd love to see you.
SALLY. Oh, I'd like to, but I won't be here.
CHRISTOPHER. Where will you be?
SALLY. I'm leaving for the Riviera tonight.
CHRISTOPHER. With whom?
SALLY. For a picture.
CHRISTOPHER. Well, splendid. Is it a good part?
SALLY. (*Rises and crosses to above* L. *of couch.*) I don't really know. I expect so. You haven't got a drink, Chris. Have a drop of this. Make it a loving cup. (*Christopher takes a sip.*) Why are you going away, Chris? (*Sits on couch.*)
CHRISTOPHER. Because I'll never write as long as I'm here. And I've got to write. It's the only thing I give a damn about. I don't regret the time I've spent here. I wouldn't have missed a single hangover of it. But now I've got to put it all down—what I think about it. And live by it, too, if I can. Thank you for the idea about that book, Sally. (*Rises and goes to* L. *of Sally.*) The short stories. I think maybe that will work out.
SALLY. Oh, I hope so, I do want you to be good, Chris. (*Puts glass down on floor and gets cigarette from bag.*)
CHRISTOPHER. I am going to try, Sally. (*Sits* L. *of Sally.*) Now, tell me about you and this job that you don't seem to know anything about. Or care about. Who's the man, Sally?
SALLY. Man? (*Lights a cigarette.*)
CHRISTOPHER. Oh, come off it.
SALLY. (*Giggling a little.*) Well, there is a man. He's wonderful, Chris. He really is.
CHRISTOPHER. Where did you meet him?

SALLY. Two days ago. Just after we left here. He saw us in the street . . . Mummy and me, I mean—and our eyes met—his and mine, I mean—and he sort of followed us. To a tea shop, where he sat and gazed at me. And back to the hotel. And at the restaurant. He had the table next to us, and he kept sort of hitching his foot around my chair. And he passed me a note in the fruit-basket. Only Mummy got it by mistake. But it was in German, I told her it was from a film producer. And I went over and talked to him, and he *was!* Then we met later. He's quite marvellous, Chris. (*Kneels on couch.*) He's got a long, black beard. Well, not really long. I've never been kissed by a beard before, I thought it would be awful. But it isn't. It's quite exciting. Only he doesn't speak much German. He's a Yugloslavian. That's why I don't know much about the picture. But I'm sure it will be all right. He'll write in something, and he's got ideas about South America later.
CHRISTOPHER. Oh, no, Sally, not South America!
SALLY. (*Rises and goes to above* R. *of couch.*) Why not? Oh, you mean brothels and things. Oh, no, darling, I'll be terribly careful, I'll take references and everything. And now I've got to go . . .
CHRISTOPHER. (*Rises.*) Oh, Sally, *must* you? Must you go on like this? Why don't you go home, too?
SALLY. And be Miss Watson-Courtneidge again?
CHRISTOPHER. Come back with me, I mean it, Sally. My family'll give me some money if I'm home. Or I'll get a job. (*Goes to Sally and puts his hand on her shoulder.*) I'll see that you're all right.
SALLY. (*Crosses to pouffe and puts cigarette out.*) It wouldn't be any good, Chris. I'd run away from you, too. The moment anything exciting came along. It's all right for you. You're a writer. You really are, I'm not even an actress, really. I'd love to see my name in lights, but even if I had a first-night tomorrow, if something attractive turned up, I'd go after it. I can't help it. That's me. You know that really, don't you? (*Christopher sits head of couch.*)
CHRISTOPHER. (*Facing Sally.*) Yes, Sally, I'm afraid I do.
SALLY. Afraid? Oh, Chris, am I too awful—for *me* I mean?
CHRISTOPHER. No, Sally. I'm very fond of you.
SALLY. I do hope you are. Because I am of you. (*Goes to Christopher.*) Was it true about eternal friendship that we swore?

CHRISTOPHER. Yes, of course it was. Really true. Tell me, do you have an address? (*Sally goes to couch and collects cloak and bag.*)
SALLY. No, I don't. But I'll write. I really will. Postcards and everything. (*Crosses to door.*) And you write to me. Of course, you'll be writing all sorts of things, books and things, that I can read. (*Turns to Christopher.*) Will you dedicate one to me?
CHRISTOPHER. The very first one.
SALLY. Oh, good. Perhaps that'll be my only claim to fame. Well, good-bye for now, Chris. Neck and leg-break.
CHRISTOPHER. Neck and leg-break. (*Christopher and Sally go into each other's arms.*)
SALLY. (*Starts to go, then turns to Christopher.*) I do love you. (*She goes, swiftly.*)
CHRISTOPHER. (*Stares after her, for a moment.*) I love you, too, Sally. And it's so damned stupid that that's not enough to keep two people together. (*Starts to move toward the window. The lights begin to dim.*) The camera's taken all its pictures, and now it's going away to develop them. I wonder how Sally will look when I've developed her? I haven't got an end for her yet, but there probably isn't one. She'll just go on and on, as she always has—somewhere. (*Looks out of the window.*) There she goes now. Into the photograph. She's just going around the corner. (*Watches as the curtain starts to fall.*) Don't forget those postcards, Sally.

CURTAIN

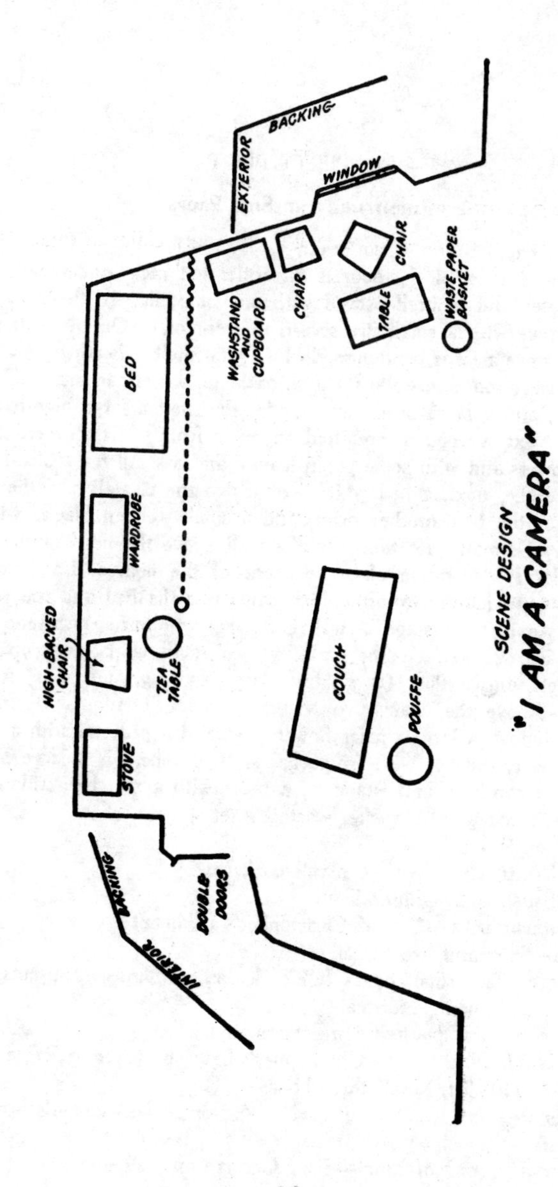
EXTERIOR BACKING
BACKING
WINDOW
CHAIR
CHAIR
TABLE
WASTE PAPER BASKET
WASHSTAND AND CUPBOARD
BED
WARDROBE
HIGH-BACKED CHAIR
TEA TABLE
COUCH
POUFFE
STOVE
DOUBLE DOORS
INTERIOR BACKING
SCENE DESIGN
"I AM A CAMERA"

PROPERTY PLOT

Furniture and Side Props

The Set, From Stage R. to Stage L.

On the wall U. S. of the door is an antler hat rack, underneath it a barometer and umbrella stand with one umbrella. To the L., a tall tiled stove with a small fire screen in front of it. On the wall next to the stove a large pendulum clock. A wall shelf beneath it on which there are (from S. R. to S. L.) a china lamb, a German army officer's helmet, and a large beer stein. Under the shelf a large high-backed chair. Next, a wooden three-fold screen in front of which there are a tall flowerstand with some green leaves, and a small tea table. Then, a wardrobe, next, a bed which extends to the L. wall. On the wall U. S. of the bed another print, and a small wooden plaque with a homey, German quotation. On the wall above the head of the bed is a large, decorative plate. In front of the bed, a draw curtain (about one-quarter closed) which can cover the bed and the wardrobe. Against the stage L. wall is a large combined washstand and cupboard, flanked on the wall by two small china dogs on wall brackets, on the floor (U. S.) by a large slop jug, and (D. S.) a side chair. Above the chair, two Medici prints (Christopher's). In the bay window, a large wicker flowerstand and a pedestal with a vase. A dome chandelier with fringe hangs U. C. There is a large pouffe D. R., a couch C. and, stage L., a table with a matching side chair above it and a small wicker waste basket stage R. of it

Pre-set on Stage

On antlers U. S. *of door*—A man's dark hat

On wall shelf U. R.—China lamb

On big chair U. R.—Top of Christopher's pajamas

On bed—Shirt and two books

On pouffe—Two small boxes full of letters, clippings, snapshots, odd papers and correspondence

On floor at L. *of pouffe*—Three German books

On couch (from R. *to* L.*)*—Christopher's bathrobe (over back), laundry tied up with list, towel, three books

On floor in front of R. *end of couch*—A pair of Christopher's bedroom slippers

On floor at L. *end of couch*—Four German magazines

On table (false top with duplicate cover)—Half a dozen books, pile of manuscript paper, check book, three bottles of pills, bottle of hard candy, ruler, letter opener, plate with crust of sandwich, half empty bottle of German beer and glass, notebook, ash tray and matches, pen and inkstand, two pencils

On floor at R. *of table*—Waste basket, lots of crumpled note-paper, half dozen German and English magazines and books

On cupboard—Two tooth glasses, practical washbowl and water pitcher, small mirror, spare thermometer, corkscrew (in case champagne cork breaks)

In cupboard—Almost finished bottle of gin (top shelf U. S.), half-full bottle of brandy (top shelf U. S.), two spare glasses (*bottom shelf* U. S.), small basket with at least three eggs (bottom shelf D. S.), bottle of Worcestershire sauce (bottom shelf D. S.), small bottle of iodine (*top shelf* D. S.), small bottle of aspirin (top shelf D. S.), flat tin of small and large plaster dressings (top shelf D. S.), shelves dressed with cans, bottles, boxes of food

In wardrobe—Three suits and a coat of Christopher's, hanging up, various clothes of Christopher's on the shelves. On the bottom shelf: tartan shirt, four bright solid color silk shirts and an old pair of drawers with a large hole. (These clothes to be covered until Act III, Scene 3)

PRE-SET OFF STAGE

Up Stage—Lace tea-cloth, three-tier cake stand with jam tarts, biscuits and napkins, tray with three coffee cups and saucers, coffee pot, creamer and sugar bowl with tongs, two-page letter from England to Sally Bowles, tray with coffee cup, saucer and coffee pot (re-set for Act III, Scene 2), clean tooth glass, envelope with a note from Clive and three hundred marks (four notes), cigarette (quarter-inch cut off), for Sally to light in Act I, Scene 1 for re-entrance, supply of cigarettes for Sally, Fritz and Christopher

Stage R.—Three parcels (the size to contain six shirts, one dozen pairs of stockings and some large bottles of perfume), enormous flower box tied with red tinsel ribbon in a large bow from "Richter," small bouquet of flowers in white tissue paper, large wicker basket containing twelve bottles of champagne. (One practical—one spare), men's suit box from "Landauer" tied with string, dress box with Sally's négligé from "Birnbaum"

FOR CHANGE TO ACT I, SCENE 2

False top, with duplicate cover, for table with: Sally's make-up, lotions, small mirror, fountain pen, powder puff, ash tray, perfumes, mascara, matches, etc., all on a large tray

In a prop basket—Small yellow doll, thermometer in case, large blue doll, teddy bear, pair of stockings, Sally's blue bedroom slippers, small red doll, "The Kitten's Awakening" picture, clean tooth glass, three slips

FOR CHANGE TO ACT II, SCENE 1

In prop basket—Sally's address book, small dictionary, pencil and paper, cigarettes and ash tray, large pillow, deck of cards, four bottles of champagne (one practical—one spare), two tooth glasses, picture album and pictures, jar of paste, matches and lighter

FOR CHANGE TO ACT II, SCENE 2

Four champagne glasses. (One scotch taped—to be broken), suitcase

IN PROP BASKET FOR CHANGE TO ACT III, SCENE 1

Three brandy glasses, one tooth glass, two dresses, house coat, pair of stockings, two slips, blue panties, pink panties, large pillow (re-set), nightdress, coffee tray with coffee cup, coffee pot and brandy glass half full

FOR CHANGE TO ACT THREE, SCENE 2

German newspaper, coffee tray, coffee cup and coffee pot (re-set from Act III, Scene 1)

FOR CHANGE TO ACT III, SCENE 3

Small trunk, bottle of gin one-eighth full, ash tray and two books

PERSONAL

SALLY—Cigarette box, cigarettes, lighter, long cigarette holder, small compact. (All to fit in her handbag)

CHRISTOPHER—Small flat tin cigarette box, cigarettes, box of matches, note case with several German marks

FRITZ—Smart cigarette case, lighter and cigarettes

NATALIA—Several calling cards

SCENE CHANGES

CHANGE TO ACT I, SCENE 2

Strike—From wall shelf U. R., china lamb; from bed, laundry and two boxes of clippings, books, and shirt; from waste basket, gin bottle; from small table, coffee tray and lace table-cloth; from antler rack, hat; from L. of lounge, three-layer cake stand

Re-set—Small table to the original position, open bed curtains

Set—On wall shelf U. R., yellow doll; on small table, large blue doll and thermometer; on cupboard, clean tooth glass and small red doll; on wall D. S. of cupboard, "Kitten's Awakening" picture; on table, false table-top with Sally's make-up tray, etc.; at head of couch, teddy bear; on couch, pair of stockings and chemise; on big chair U. R., slip; over foot of bed, slip; in front of bed, Sally's slippers

CHANGE TO ACT II, SCENE 1

Strike—From table, three packages and dirty tooth glass; from closet, all Christopher's clothes except from bottom shelf; from lounge, flower box ribbon; from cupboard, letter-opener, thermometer and dirty tooth glass

Re-set—Table to C. position, couch to S. L. position, pouffe to between table and lounge, large chair to S. R. of table, chair from above table with Sally's make-up tray, to position U. R., small table to S. L. of lounge, waste basket to above small table, blue doll to the bed, Worcestershire sauce back to cupboard

Set—On table, Sally's address book, dictionary, note-paper, pencil, ash tray and matches; on cupboard, two clean tooth glasses; in cupboard, four bottles of champagne (one practical, one spare); on couch (at head), large pillow; on couch (at foot), cards laid out for game of patience; on small table, Sally's cigarettes, lighter and ash tray and matches; on pouffe, picture album and three snapshots; on floor, R. of pouffe, large jar of paste; extra side chair, with high back, to S. L. of table, leave door open

CHANGE TO ACT II, SCENE 2

Strike—From lounge, large pillow; from small table, deck of cards; from chair D. S. of cupboard, album and jar of paste; from U. R., wicker champagne basket; from table, champagne bottle, three glasses and cork

Re-set—Small table to original position, towel from table to rack on cupboard, address book and dictionary to small table

Set—In front of bed, open suitcase, Sally's slippers; on cupboard, four champagne glasses (one scotch taped)

CHANGE TO ACT III, SCENE 1

Strike—From in front of bed, suitcase; from bed, négligé box, négligé, large blue doll, Sally's pink gloves and money; from lounge, teddy bear and suit box; from cupboard, champagne glasses and bottle; from in cupboard, champagne bottles; from table, champagne glass, note-paper, pencil and dictionary; extra chair

Re-set—Table, lounge, pouffe, waste basket, table chair, and large chair to Act I positions, bath towels to rack on cupboard, Sally's hat to couch, Sally's shoes to in front of couch, make-up tray to table, Sally's bag to L. of make-up tray, ash tray to S. R. of make-up tray, silver-backed hairbrush from make-up tray to cupboard

Set—In wardrobe, hang three or four dresses (leave S. R. door open); on pouffe, green dress; over fire screen, white slip; over screen, blue panties and stockings; over foot of bed, pink panties; over curtain rod, blue flowered dress; in front of bed, white bed pillow; bed, completely mussed, nightdress; on floor, R. of cupboard, blue house coat; on cupboard (hanging U. S.), blue slip; on cupboard, three brandy glasses and a tooth glass; on table (D. R. corner), tray with large coffee pot, cup, saucer and half full brandy glass; on floor, between lounge and table, Sally's skirt; at foot of lounge, Sally's jacket; on small table, Christopher's article

CHANGE TO ACT III, SCENE 2

Strike—From table, false table-top with make-up tray, etc.; from wall D. S. of cupboard, "The Kitten's Awakening" picture; all Sally's dolls, clothes, etc., from room

Set—On table, false table-top with Christopher's books, etc.; on table (D. R. corner), tray with coffee cup, saucer and coffee pot (re-set from previous scene without brandy glass); on wall D. S. of cupboard, Christopher's two pictures; on couch, German newspaper; close wardrobe door; close bed curtains

CHANGE TO ACT III, SCENE 3

Strike—From table, plaster dressings, iodine, coffee tray, brandy bottle and glasses; from couch, German newspaper

Re-set—Water pitcher in bowl

Set—S. L. of lounge, small trunk (open and facing U. S.); on cupboard, gin bottle one-third full; on pouffe, two books and an ash tray; open bed curtains to foot of bed; open S. L. wardrobe door

NEW PLAYS

★ **HONOUR by Joanna Murray-Smith.** In a series of intense confrontations, a wife, husband, lover and daughter negotiate the forces of passion, history, responsibility and honour. "HONOUR makes for surprisingly interesting viewing. Tight, crackling dialogue (usually played out in punchy verbal duels) captures characters unable to deal with emotions … Murray-Smith effectively places her characters in situations that strip away pretense." *–Variety* "… the play's virtues are strong: a distinctive theatrical voice, passionate concerns … HONOUR might just capture a few honors of its own." *–Time Out Magazine* [1M, 3W] ISBN: 0-8222-1683-3

★ **MR. PETERS' CONNECTIONS by Arthur Miller.** Mr. Miller describes the protagonist as existing in a dream-like state when the mind is "freed to roam from real memories to conjectures, from trivialities to tragic insights, from terror of death to glorying in one's being alive." With this memory play, the Tony Award and Pulitzer Prize-winner reaffirms his stature as the world's foremost dramatist. "… a cross between Joycean stream-of-consciousness and Strindberg's dream plays, sweetened with a dose of William Saroyan's philosophical whimsy … CONNECTIONS is most intriguing …" *–The NY Times* [5M, 3W] ISBN: 0-8222-1687-6

★ **THE WAITING ROOM by Lisa Loomer.** Three women from different centuries meet in a doctor's waiting room in this dark comedy about the timeless quest for beauty – and its cost. "… THE WAITING ROOM … is a bold, risky melange of conflicting elements that is … terrifically moving … There's no resisting the fierce emotional pull of the play." *–The NY Times* "… one of the high points of this year's Off-Broadway season … THE WAITING ROOM is well worth a visit." *–Back Stage* [7M, 4W, flexible casting] ISBN: 0-8222-1594-2

★ **THE OLD SETTLER by John Henry Redwood.** A sweet-natured comedy about two church-going sisters in 1943 Harlem and the handsome young man who rents a room in their apartment. "For all of its decent sentiments, THE OLD SETTLER avoids sentimentality. It has the authenticity and lack of pretense of an Early American sampler." *–The NY Times* "We've had some fine plays Off-Broadway this season, and this is one of the best." *–The NY Post* [1M, 3W] ISBN: 0-8-222-1642-6

★ **LAST TRAIN TO NIBROC by Arlene Hutton.** In 1940 two young strangers share a seat on a train bound east only to find their paths will cross again. "All aboard. LAST TRAIN TO NIBROC is a sweetly told little chamber romance." *–Show Business* "… [a] gently charming little play, reminiscent of Thornton Wilder in its look at rustic Americans who are to be treasured for their simplicity and directness …" *–Associated Press* "The old formula of boy wins girls, boy loses girl, boy wins girl still works … [a] well-made play that perfectly captures a slice of small-town-life-gone-by." *–Back Stage* [1M, 1W] ISBN: 0-8222-1753-8

★ **OVER THE RIVER AND THROUGH THE WOODS by Joe DiPietro.** Nick sees both sets of his grandparents every Sunday for dinner. This is routine until he has to tell them that he's been offered a dream job in Seattle. The news doesn't sit so well. "A hilarious family comedy that is even funnier than his long running musical revue *I Love You, You're Perfect, Now Change.*" *–Back Stage* "Loaded with laughs every step of the way." *–Star-Ledger* [3M, 3W] ISBN: 0-8222-1712-0

★ **SIDE MAN by Warren Leight.** 1999 Tony Award winner. This is the story of a broken family and the decline of jazz as popular entertainment. "… a tender, deeply personal memory play about the turmoil in the family of a jazz musician as his career crumbles at the dawn of the age of rock-and-roll …" *–The NY Times* "[SIDE MAN] is an elegy for two things – a lost world and a lost love. When the two notes sound together in harmony, it is moving and graceful …" *–The NY Daily News* "An atmospheric memory play … with crisp dialogue and clearly drawn characters … reflects the passing of an era with persuasive insight … The joy and despair of the musicians is skillfully illustrated." *–Variety* [5M, 3W] ISBN: 0-8222-1721-X

NEW PLAYS

★ **CLOSER by Patrick Marber.** Winner of the 1998 Olivier Award for Best Play and the 1999 New York Drama Critics Circle Award for Best Foreign Play. Four lives intertwine over the course of four and a half years in this densely plotted, stinging look at modern love and betrayal. "CLOSER is a sad, savvy, often funny play that casts a steely, unblinking gaze at the world of relationships and lets you come to your own conclusions ... CLOSER does not merely hold your attention; it burrows into you." *–New York Magazine* "A powerful, darkly funny play about the cosmic collision between the sun of love and the comet of desire." *–Newsweek Magazine* [2M, 2W] ISBN: 0-8222-1722-8

★ **THE MOST FABULOUS STORY EVER TOLD by Paul Rudnick.** A stage manager, headset and prompt book at hand, brings the house lights to half, then dark, and cues the creation of the world. Throughout the play, she's in control of everything. In other words, she's either God, or she thinks she is. "Line by line, Mr. Rudnick may be the funniest writer for the stage in the United States today ... One-liners, epigrams, withering put-downs and flashing repartee: These are the candles that Mr. Rudnick lights instead of cursing the darkness ... a testament to the virtues of laughing ... and in laughter, there is something like the memory of Eden." *–The NY Times* "Funny it is ... consistently, rapaciously, deliriously ... easily the funniest play in town." *–Variety* [4M, 5W] ISBN: 0-8222-1720-1

★ **A DOLL'S HOUSE by Henrik Ibsen, adapted by Frank McGuinness.** Winner of the 1997 Tony Award for Best Revival. "New, raw, gut-twisting and gripping. Easily the hottest drama this season." *–USA Today* "Bold, brilliant and alive." *–The Wall Street Journal* "A thunderclap of an evening that takes your breath away." *–Time Magazine* [4M, 4W, 2 boys] ISBN: 0-8222-1636-1

★ **THE HERBAL BED by Peter Whelan.** The play is based on actual events which occurred in Stratford-upon-Avon in the summer of 1613, when William Shakespeare's elder daughter was publicly accused of having a sexual liaison with a married neighbor and family friend. "In his probing new play, THE HERBAL BED ... Peter Whelan muses about a sidelong event in the life of Shakespeare's family and creates a finely textured tapestry of love and lies in the early 17th-century Stratford." *–The NY Times* "It is a first rate drama with interesting moral issues of truth and expediency." *–The NY Post* [5M, 3W] ISBN: 0-8222-1675-2

★ **SNAKEBIT by David Marshall Grant.** A study of modern friendship when put to the test. "... a rather smart and absorbing evening of water-cooler theater, the intimate sort of Off-Broadway experience that has you picking apart the recognizable characters long after the curtain calls." *– The NY Times* "Off-Broadway keeps on presenting us with compelling reasons for going to the theater. The latest is SNAKEBIT, David Marshall Grant's smart new comic drama about being thirtysomething and losing one's way in life." *–The NY Daily News* [3M, 1W] ISBN: 0-8222-1724-4

★ **A QUESTION OF MERCY by David Rabe.** The Obie Award-winning playwright probes the sensitive and controversial issue of doctor-assisted suicide in the age of AIDS in this poignant drama. "There are many devastating ironies in Mr. Rabe's beautifully considered, piercingly clear-eyed work ..." *–The NY Times* "With unsettling candor and disturbing insight, the play arouses pity and understanding of a troubling subject ... Rabe's provocative tale is an affirmation of dignity that rings clear and true." *–Variety* [6M, 1W] ISBN: 0-8222-1643-4

★ **DIMLY PERCEIVED THREATS TO THE SYSTEM by Jon Klein.** Reality and fantasy overlap with hilarious results as this unforgettable family attempts to survive the nineties. "Here's a play whose point about fractured families goes to the heart, mind – and ears." *–The Washington Post* "... an end-of-the millennium comedy about a family on the verge of a nervous breakdown ... Trenchant and hilarious ..." *–The Baltimore Sun* [2M, 4W] ISBN: 0-8222-1677-9

NEW PLAYS

★ **AS BEES IN HONEY DROWN by Douglas Carter Beane.** Winner of the John Gassner Playwriting Award. A hot young novelist finds the subject of his new screenplay in a New York socialite who leads him into the world of *Auntie Mame* and *Breakfast at Tiffany's*, before she takes him for a ride. "A delicious soufflé of a satire … [an] extremely entertaining fable for an age that always chooses image over substance." *–The NY Times* "… A witty assessment of one of the most active and relentless industries in a consumer society … the creation of 'hot' young things, which the media have learned to mass produce with efficiency and zeal." *–The NY Daily News* [3M, 3W, flexible casting] ISBN: 0-8222-1651-5

★ **STUPID KIDS by John C. Russell.** In rapid, highly stylized scenes, the story follows four high-school students as they make their way from first through eighth period and beyond, struggling with the fears, frustrations, and longings peculiar to youth. "In STUPID KIDS … playwright John C. Russell gets the opera of adolescence to a T … The stylized teenspeak of STUPID KIDS … suggests that Mr. Russell may have hidden a tape recorder under a desk in study hall somewhere and then scoured the tapes for good quotations … it is the kids' insular, ceaselessly churning world, a pre-adult world of Doritos and libidos, that the playwright seeks to lay bare." *–The NY Times* "STUPID KIDS [is] a sharp-edged … whoosh of teen angst and conformity anguish. It is also very funny." *–NY Newsday* [2M, 2W] ISBN: 0-8222-1698-1

★ **COLLECTED STORIES by Donald Margulies.** From Obie Award-winner Donald Margulies comes a provocative analysis of a student-teacher relationship that turns sour when the protégé becomes a rival. "With his fine ear for detail, Margulies creates an authentic, insular world, and he gives equal weight to the opposing viewpoints of two formidable characters." *–The LA Times* "This is probably Margulies' best play to date …" *–The NY Post* "… always fluid and lively, the play is thick with ideas, like a stock-pot of good stew." *–The Village Voice* [2W] ISBN: 0-8222-1640-X

★ **FREEDOMLAND by Amy Freed.** An overdue showdown between a son and his father sets off fireworks that illuminate the neurosis, rage and anxiety of one family – and of America at the turn of the millennium. "FREEDOMLAND's more obvious links are to *Buried Child* and *Bosoms and Neglect*. Freed, like Guare, is an inspired wordsmith with a gift for surreal touches in situations grounded in familiar and real territory." *–Curtain Up* [3M, 4W] ISBN: 0-8222-1719-8

★ **STOP KISS by Diana Son.** A poignant and funny play about the ways, both sudden and slow, that lives can change irrevocably. "There's so much that is vital and exciting about STOP KISS … you want to embrace this young author and cheer her onto other works … the writing on display here is funny and credible … you also will be charmed by its heartfelt characters and up-to-the-minute humor." *–The NY Daily News* "… irresistibly exciting … a sweet, sad, and enchantingly sincere play." *–The NY Times* [3M, 3W] ISBN: 0-8222-1731-7

★ **THREE DAYS OF RAIN by Richard Greenberg.** The sins of fathers and mothers make for a bittersweet elegy in this poignant and revealing drama. "… a work so perfectly judged it heralds the arrival of a major playwright … Greenberg is extraordinary." *–The NY Daily News* "Greenberg's play is filled with graceful passages that are by turns melancholy, harrowing, and often, quite funny." *–Variety* [2M, 1W] ISBN: 0-8222-1676-0

★ **THE WEIR by Conor McPherson.** In a bar in rural Ireland, the local men swap spooky stories in an attempt to impress a young woman from Dublin who recently moved into a nearby "haunted" house. However, the tables are soon turned when she spins a yarn of her own. "You shed all sense of time at this beautiful and devious new play." *–The NY Times* "Sheer theatrical magic. I have rarely been so convinced that I have just seen a modern classic. Tremendous." *–The London Daily Telegraph* [4M, 1W] ISBN: 0-8222-1706-6